你好

Nǐ Hǎo

②

Chinese Language Course
Elementary Level

by

Shumang Fredlein ● Paul Fredlein

ChinaSoft

Nǐ Hǎo 2 – **Chinese Language Course** – **Elementary Level**

First Published 1993; reprinted 1994, 1995, 1997, 1999

New edition 2002; reprinted 2003, 2005, 2006, 2007

ChinaSoft Pty Ltd   ABN: 61 083 458 459

P.O. Box 845, Toowong, Brisbane, Qld 4066, AUSTRALIA

Telephone (61-7) 3371-7436

Facsimile   (61-7) 3371-6711

www.chinasoft.com.au

Written by Shumang Fredlein (林淑满) & Paul Fredlein

Cover and Illustrations by Zhengdong Su (苏正东) & Xiaolin Xue (薛晓林)

Edited by Sitong Jan (詹絲桐)

Typeset by ChinaSoft on Apple Macintosh

Printed in Australia by Watson Ferguson & Company, Brisbane

Companion workbook, audio CDs and Games software also available

ISBN 978 1 876739 12 6

Introduction

你好 Nǐ Hǎo is a basic course for beginning students of Chinese. It introduces Chinese language and culture and aims to teach communication in both spoken and written Chinese. The objectives are to enable students to use Chinese in the classroom, playground, local community and countries where the Chinese language is spoken.

The text is richly illustrated, providing a stimulating language learning tool to motivate students. Characters are used throughout the text to enhance the students' reading and writing ability. Pinyin only acts as a guide to pronunciation. When it appears on top of the characters, no capital letter is used at the beginning of the sentence and no full stop is employed. As learning progresses, the Pinyin of the characters that students have learnt is omitted. To equip students to read authentic materials, various print fonts are used: Kǎishū [楷书], used in the main text, is an ideal font for students to learn to write; Sòngtǐ [宋体], used in the sentence patterns, is a font commonly used in newspapers and general publications; while Hēitǐ [黑体] is only used for titles. Apart from print fonts, various hand-written scripts are included to provide students with the opportunity to read handwriting. To make students aware of the current use of traditional characters in Taiwan and overseas Chinese communities, the traditional form is included in the vocabulary list in Appendix 1.

Each unit of the text in this book includes the subsections: *Illustrated texts, Learn the sentences, New words and expressions, Write the characters* and *Something to know.* In *Illustrated texts*, each conversation is based on daily life with the language in a spiralled structure. The illustrations assist in the interpretation of the conversation and are ideally suited to role playing. Grammar explanations in *Learn the sentences* are simple and illustrated with examples to clarify usage. Students can also use this section to hold conversations with partners. In *New words and expressions*, the meaning of the separate characters in each word will assist students to understand the structure of the word. Characters that the students should learn to write have the stroke order clearly illustrated in *Write the characters*. It is essential to write characters in the correct stroke order. Culture related to the content of the lesson is introduced in *Something to know*, a section designed to enrich cultural understanding and generate interest in learning the language.

In addition to the five subsections, cartoons, jokes, riddles and little stories also play important roles in the book. They are light and cheerful materials offering wonderful opportunities for practice and reinforcement.

For students who wish to learn traditional characters, the traditional character edition is published by Cheng & Tsui Company in the USA under licence from ChinaSoft.

Contents

Introduction iii

Map of China vi

<div dì yī kè wǒ de shēngrì>

第一课　我的生日　(My birthday) 1

(1) What is the date? (2) What day is it today? (3) Today is my birthday

<div dì èr kè wǒ de rìcháng shēnghuó>

第二课　我的日常生活　(My daily routine) 16

(1) What are you doing? (2) What time is it? (3) What is your daily routine?
(4) You are late

<div dì sān kè Xiǎomíng de jiā>

第三课　小明的家　(Xiaoming's home) 29

(1) Where are they? (2) House plan (3) What happened? (4) Xiaoming's Sunday

<div dì sì kè wǒ de yīfu>

第四课　我的衣服　(My clothes) 43

(1) What clothes do they wear? (2) Do they fit? (3) What should I wear?
(4) Where are my shoes?

<div dì wǔ kè mǎi dōngxi>

第五课　买东西　(Shopping) 55

(1) How much is it? (2) In the department store (3) In the bookshop (4) At the market

dì liù kè   bàifǎng péngyou
第六课 拜访朋友 (Visiting a friend).......................................70

(1) Inviting (2) Visiting (3) Introducing (4) Leaving

dì qī kè   dǎ diànhuà
第七课 打电话 (Making phone calls) 82

(1) A wrong number (2) Not home (3) Wait a moment please (4) Speaking

dì bā kè   chī fàn
第八课 吃饭 (Eating) 93

*(1) A note to a friend (2) We often go to a restaurant (3) Eating at the restaurant
(4) Eating at home*

dì jiǔ kè   tiānqì
第九课 天气 (Weather)..105

*(1) What's the weather today? (2) Beijing's weather (3) Weather report
(4) It is raining again*

dì shí kè   fùxí
第十课 复习 (Revision) 116

(1) A diary (2) Language functions

Appendices 120

*(1) Words and expressioons (Chinese-English) (2) Words and expressioons (English-
Chinese) (3) Learn to write (by lesson)*

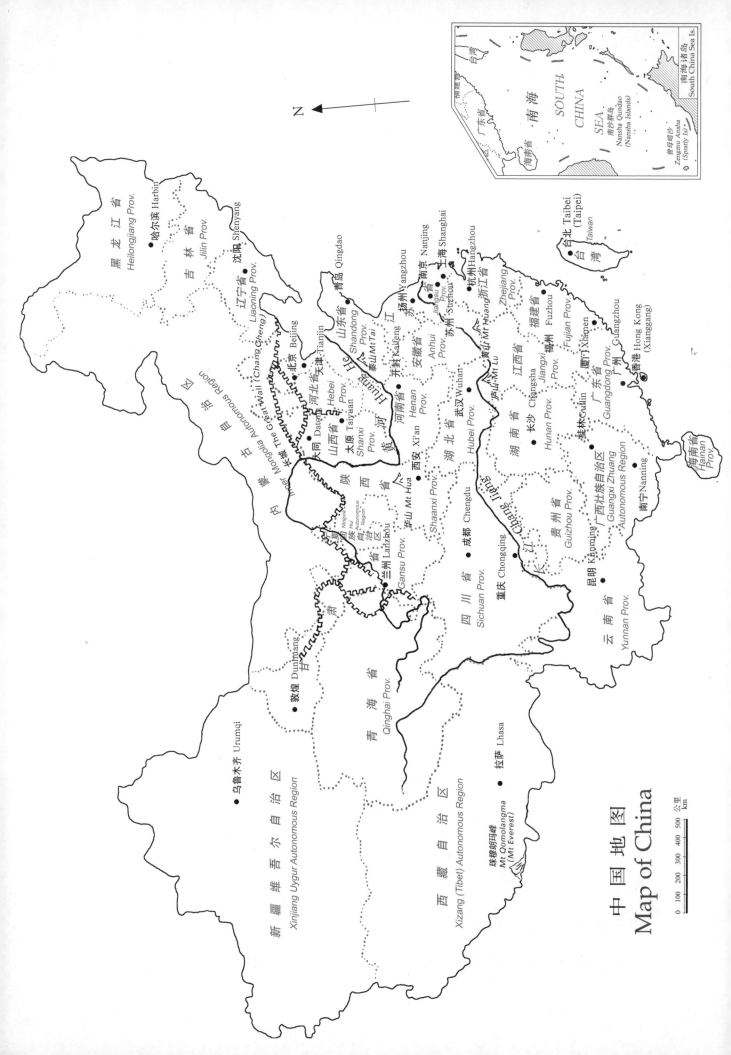

中国地图
Map of China

dì　yī　kè　wǒ　de　shēngrì
第 一 课 我 的 生 日

1 What is the date?

Lánlan　jīntiān　　　yuè　hào
兰兰，今天是不是三月十七号？

不是。

nà me　　jīntiān jǐ yuè jǐ hào
那么，今天几月几号？

今天是三月十八号。
zuótiān
昨天是三月十七号。
míngtiān
明天是三月十九号。
hòutiān
后天是……

Hǎo le　　　zhīdao
好了！好了！我知道了。
hòutiān　　　　duì
后天是三月二十号，对不对？

cuò
对……没错。

② What day is today?

mā　míngtiān hé Dàwěi qù diàoyú　kěyǐ
妈，我明天和大伟去钓鱼，可以吗？

xíng　　yào shàng xué
不行！明天要上学！

yí　　xīngqī
咦！今天星期几？

今天星期四，明天星期五。

ò　　yǐwéi
哦！我以为今天是星期五，明天是星期六。

cuò le　　hòutiān
你错了。后天是星期六。

TUE	WED	THU	FRI	SAT
前天	昨天	今天	明天	后天

diàoyú
那么，我星期六去钓鱼，可以吗？

那么星期日可以吗？

yào　　mǎi dōngxi
也不行。你星期六要和我去买东西。

dàgài
大概可以吧！

3 Today is my birthday

> Dàwěi
> 大伟，今天是五月十四日。

> zhīdao nián
> 我知道。今天是二〇〇二年
> 五月十四日，星期二。

> shēngrì zhīdao
> 今天是我的生日，你知道吗？

> ō a nǎ shēng
> 喔！真的啊！你是哪年生的？

> ne
> 我是一九九〇年生的。你呢？

> 我也是一九九〇年生的。

> 你的生日是几月几号？

> 我的生日是七月十六号。

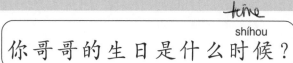

你哥哥的生日是什么时候？

他的生日也是七月十六号。

你们的生日是同一天啊？

是啊！我们是双胞胎。

来，请你吃我的生日蛋糕。

谢谢你。祝你生日快乐。

Learn the sentences

※ **Asking the date**

To ask *What's the date today?* say 今天是几号? Jīntiān shì jǐ hào? or say 今天是几月几号? Jīntiān shì jǐ yuè jǐ hào? or more formally say 今天是几月几日? Jīntiān shì jǐ yuè jǐ rì? To answer, replace the question word 几 jǐ with the number of the day and month. As 今天 Jīntiān is the subject of the sentence, it is placed at the beginning. The Chinese like to use the concept of big to small. Dates begin with the year, followed by the month and finally the day. In spoken Chinese, the verb 是 shì is often omitted, but can be used for emphasis.

今天是几号？	今天是二十五号。
今天几号？	今天十九号。
今天是几月几号？	今天是三月七号。
今天几月几号？	十一月四号。
今天是几月几日？	今天是六月十八日。

To ask about yesterday's or tomorrow's date, replace 今天 jīntiān with 昨天 zuótiān or 明天 míngtiān. In Chinese, as tense is shown by the time stated, i.e. yesterday or tomorrow, the verb does not change for future or past tense.

zuótiān 昨天是几月几号？	昨天是九月四号。
qiántiān 前天是几月几号？	前天是九月三号。
明天是几月几号？	明天是九月六号。
hòutiān 后天几月几号？	后天九月七号。

✳ **Asking the day of the week**

To ask What day is it today? say 今天是星期几？Jīntiān shì xīngqī jǐ? To answer, replace the question word 几 jǐ with the number of the day. The Chinese use the numbers one to six for Monday to Saturday and 天 tiān or 日 rì for Sunday. Again, the verb 是 shì, which is used in written Chinese, is often omitted in spoken Chinese, but can be used for emphasis. To ask about yesterday or tomorrow, use the same sentence structure, but replace 今天 jīntiān with 昨天 zuótiān for yesterday or 明天 míngtiān for tomorrow.

今天是星期几？	今天是星期五。
昨天是星期几？	昨天是星期四。
qiántiān 前天是星期几？	前天是星期三。
明天星期几？	明天星期六。
hòutiān 后天星期几？	后天是星期日。
	后天星期天。

✳ **Asking the year someone was born**

To ask What year were you born? say 你是哪年生的？Nǐ shì nǎ nián shēng de? To answer, replace the question word 哪 nǎ with the number of the year.

nǎ 你是哪年生的？	我是一九六七年生的。
他是哪年生的？	他是一九五八年生的。
她是哪年生的？	她是一九八四年生的。
你姐姐是哪年生的？	她是一九七六年生的。

✳ **Confirming a date**

To ask someone to confirm a date, use 是不是 shì bú shì in the question. To answer yes, say 是 shì; to answer no, say 不是 bú shì.

今天是不是三月五日？	是。
明天是不是七月十八日？	不是。
昨天是不是十月一号？	昨天不是十月一号。

✳ **Asking if something is correct**

To ask Is it right? say 对不对 duì bú duì. To answer yes, say 对 duì; to answer no, say 不对 bú duì.

今天是五月六日，对不对？	对。
明天是五月七日，对不对？	对。
昨天是五月三日，对不对？	不对。

✳ **Seeking permission**

To ask for permission to do something, state the activity followed by 可以吗 kěyǐ ma. To give permission, say 可以 kěyǐ. To deny permission, say 不可以 bù kěyǐ or 不行 bù xíng. In spoken Chinese, 不行 bù xíng is used more often than 不可以 bù kěyǐ.

我明天去打球，可以吗？	可以。
我后天去游泳，可以吗？ hòutiān　　yóuyǒng	不可以。
我和爸爸去钓鱼，可以吗？ diàoyú	不行。

8

✳ Asking about birthdays

To ask When is your birthday? say 你的生日是几月几日？ Nǐ de shēngrì shì jǐ yuè jǐ rì? To answer, replace the question word 几 jǐ with the number of the month and of the day. Another way to ask is 你的生日是什么时候？ Nǐ de shēngrì shì shénme shíhou?

你的生日是几月几日？	我的生日是二月八日。
他的生日是几月几号？	他的生日是十二月一号。
你哥哥的生日是什么时候？ *shíhou*	他的生日是十月四日。

✳ Stating the date

To state a date, start with the year 年 nián, followed by the month 月 yuè, the day 日 rì and finally the day of the week 星期 xīngqī.

今天是一九九三年二月二十五日，星期四。
昨天是一九九三年二月二十四日，星期三。
明天是一九九三年二月二十六日，星期五。

New words and expressions

今天	jīntiān	today　jīn- present (time); tiān- day, sky
月	yuè	month; the moon
号	hào	date; number
那么	nàme	then　nà- that, then (*conj.*)
昨天	zuótiān	yesterday　zuó- yesterday; tiān- day, sky
明天	míngtiān	tomorrow　míng- bright; tiān- day, sky
后天	hòutiān	the day after tomorrow　hòu- after, behind
好了好了	hǎo le hǎo le	that's enough (to stop people from doing something)
了	le	[grammatical word] (There are many ways of using le. For details, see the explanation in Lesson 2, p. 23.)
对	duì	right, correct
错	cuò	wrong, incorrect
钓鱼	diàoyú	to fish　diào- to fish with a hook and line; yú- fish
可以	kěyǐ	can, may　kě- may, approve; yǐ- to use
行	xíng	all right, O.K.
要	yào	to be going to; to want
上学	shàngxué	to go to school　shàng- to go to, up; xué- to study
星期	xīngqī	week　xīng- star; qī- a period of time
哦	ò	oh [to indicate realization]
以为	yǐwéi	thought (mistakenly)　yǐ- to use; wéi- to do
买	mǎi	to buy
日	rì	day; the sun
喔	ō	oh [to express surprise/understanding]
生	shēng	to be born, to give birth to; pupil
时候	shíhou	time, moment
同	tóng	same; together
双胞胎	shuāngbāotāi	twins　shuāng- pair; bāo- born of the same parents; tāi- foetus
来	lái	to come
请	qǐng	to invite; please
蛋糕	dàngāo	cake　dàn- egg; gāo- cake, pudding

Days of the week

星期一	xīngqīyī	Monday
星期二	xīngqī'èr	Tuesday
星期三	xīngqīsān	Wednesday
星期四	xīngqīsì	Thursday
星期五	xīngqīwǔ	Friday
星期六	xīngqīliù	Saturday
星期日	xīngqīrì	Sunday
星期天	xīngqītiān	Sunday

About the week

上上（个）星期	shàng shàng (gè) xīngqī	the week before last
上（个）星期	shàng (gè) xīngqī	last week
这（个）星期	zhè (gè) xīngqī	this week
下（个）星期	xià (gè) xīngqī	next week
下下（个）星期	xià xià (gè) xīngqī	the week after next

About the month

上上个月	shàng shàng gè yuè	the month before last
上个月	shàng gè yuè	last month
这个月	zhè gè yuè	this month
下个月	xià gè yuè	next month
下下个月	xià xià gè yuè	the month after next

About the day

前天	qiántiān	the day before yesterday
昨天	zuótiān	yesterday
今天	jīntiān	today
明天	míngtiān	tomorrow
后天	hòutiān	the day after tomorrow

About the year

前年	qiánnián	the year before last
去年	qùnián	last year
今年	jīnnián	this year
明年	míngnián	next year
后年	hòunián	the year after next

Write the characters

月	日	号	今	明
yuè	rì	hào	jīn	míng
month; the moon	*day; the sun*	*date, number*	*present (time)*	*bright*
昨	天	星	期	对
zuó	tiān	xīng	qī	duì
yesterday	*day; sky*	*star*	*a period of time*	*right, correct*
错	可	以	行	生
cuò	kě	yǐ	xíng	shēng
wrong, incorrect	*may, approve*	*to use*	*all right, O.K.*	*to be born, to give birth to*

everyoneloveswangli·everyoneloveswangli·everyoneloveswangli·everyoneloveswangli·everyoneloveswangli·everyoneloveswangli·everyoneloveswangli·everyoneloveswangli·everyoneloveswangli·everyoneloveswangli·everyoneloveswangli·everyoneloveswangli·everyoneloveswangli·

王 利

王利是一九八七年生的，今年十五岁。
他是美国人，他爸爸是中国人，妈妈是
英国人。王利汉语说得很好。他喜欢踢
足球，也喜欢钓鱼。

明天是星期六，
王利要和他爸爸去
钓鱼。后天星期日是王利的生日。王利不
喜欢他的生日；他的生日是二月二十九
日。王利有一个妹妹，今年十三岁。他妹
妹也不喜欢她的生日；她的生日是十二月
二十五日。

Something to know

❀ Chinese calendar

Since the establishment of the republic in 1912, the solar calendar has been adopted as the official calendar and all official events and holidays are practised accordingly. However, the traditional lunar calendar, also called the agricultural calendar, is still used especially in rural areas. The lunar calendar is calculated according to the phases of the moon. A lunar month is the interval between new moons with a cycle of 29 or 30 days. There are 12 lunar months in a year with 13 months around every four years.

The calendar used today in China and Taiwan has the lunar date in small print beside the solar date, with some agricultural hints and weather indications. The current lunar month is printed on the first day of the month. The lunar dates from the first day to the 10th day have the word chū 初, which means beginning, placed before the number. From the 21st day to the 29th day, the symbol 廿, which is read as èrshí, is used instead of 二十.

二○○二年　二月　　　　　　壬午年

星期日	星期一	星期二	星期三	星期四	星期五	星期六
					1 二十	*2* 廿一
3 廿二	*4* 立春	*5* 廿四	*6* 廿五	*7* 廿六	*8* 廿七	*9* 廿八
10 廿九	*11* 三十	*12* 正月	*13* 初二	*14* 初三	*15* 初四	*16* 初五
17 初六	*18* 初七	*19* 雨水	*20* 初九	*21* 初十	*22* 十一	*23* 十二
24 十三	*25* 十四	*26* 十五	*27* 十六	*28* 十七		

✿ Official holidays

Official holidays are dated in accordance with the solar calendar. Some major celebrations are: (* public holidays)

China			*Taiwan*		
* 1月	1日	New Year's Day	* 1月	1日	New Year's Day
* 5月	1日	Labour Day	3月	29日	Youth Day
5月	4日	Youth Day	4月	4日	Women & Children's Day
6月	1日	Children's Day	9月	28日	Confucius' Birthday (Teacher's Day)
9月	10日	Teacher's Day	*10月	10日	National Day
*10月	1日	National Day	12月	25日	Constitution Day

✿ Traditional festivals

Although the solar calendar has been adopted as the official calendar, most Chinese traditional festivals are celebrated in accordance with the lunar calendar. The three most important festivals celebrated are the Spring Festival, the Dragon Boat Festival and the Mid-Autumn Festival. Christmas and Easter are not widely observed except by some Christians.

1. Spring Festival, chūnjié 春节, first day of the first lunar month

Chūnjié 春节, traditionally called dànián 大年 or guònián 过年, is the most important and popular festival to the Chinese. During chūnjié, northern Chinese eat jiǎozi 饺子 (dumpling) and southern Chinese eat niángāo 年糕 (sweet cake) to celebrate the festival. Words of blessing are written on red paper, called chūnlián 春联, and pasted on the door for good luck. Firecrackers are lit to dispel bad luck. On Chinese New Year's Eve, all family members return to the family house to have a feast called niányèfàn 年夜饭. A whole cooked fish is always placed on dinner table as the word *fish*

鱼 and the verb *to spare* 余 have the same pronunciation - yú, and so the expression niánnián yǒu yú 年年有余, implying that one wishes there will always be something to spare every year, is represented by the presence of the fish. After dinner, the children will receive yāsuìqián 压岁钱, money from the elder members of the family, representing the wish that they will grow well in the coming year. On New

Year's Day, people dress in their best clothes to visit friends and say congratulations, gōngxǐ 恭喜 or Happy New Year, xīnnián hǎo 新年好, to each other.

Chūnjié lasts a few days and formally ends with the Lantern Festival, Yuánxiāojié 元宵节, on the 15th day of the month. Nowadays, however, most people return to work much earlier. On the night of Yuánxiāojié children carry lanterns, dēnglóng 灯笼, outdoors and people visit temples or public places to admire the lantern displays. The lantern display is a spectacular event, especially in Taiwan.

There is a legend about the origin of the New Year's celebration. Long ago, in a village, a savage beast came out of a deep forest on the last day of every year to feed on the villagers and their domestic animals. People found out that the beast was afraid of the colour red and loud noises, so they pasted the red couplets, chūnlián, on the doors and lit firecrackers, biānpào 鞭炮, to scare it away.

People saying Happy New Year to each other and children lighting firecrackers

Dragon boat race

2. Dragon Boat Festival, Duānwǔjié 端午节, fifth day of the fifth lunar month

It is said that the Dragon Boat Festival, Duānwǔjié 端午节, is celebrated to commemorate the patriotic poet Qū Yuán 屈原, who drowned himself in the river Mìluó Jiāng 汨罗江, in the fourth century B.C.. Qū Yuán was an official who was exiled to a distant place by the king of Chǔ 楚, who refused to take his suggestions. He was so disheartened that he tied himself to a rock and drowned himself in the river. People sailed their boats out to try to rescue him, but without success. They then threw rice into the river hoping that the fish would eat the rice instead of his body. The customs of dragon boat racing and eating zòngzi 粽子, sticky rice wrapped in bamboo leaves, are believed to have originated to commemorate his death.

3. Mid-Autumn Festival, Zhōngqiūjié 中秋节, 15th day of the eighth lunar month

This festival is also known as *the Moon Festival*. Because the lunar month starts on a new moon, it is always a full moon on this festival. On this day, people enjoy sitting outdoors admiring the full moon while eating moon cakes, yuèbǐng 月饼, and fruits such as pomelo, yòuzi 柚子.

Cháng'é 嫦娥 flying to the moon after taking pills of immortality

There is a legend that thousands of years ago, there were 10 suns in the sky and it was burning hot on earth. An archer, Hòuyì 后羿, bravely shot down nine of the suns and saved the earth from famine. He was beloved among the people, and they made him a king. He was also awarded pills of immortality by the goddess Wángmǔ Niángniang 王母娘娘. The pills were for both him and his wife Cháng'é 嫦娥, but Cháng'é was curious and could not resist the temptation of immortality. She secretly took all the pills herself, which not only made her immortal but also floated her to the moon to live forever.

dì　èr　kè　wǒ　de　rìcháng　shēnghuó
第 二 课　我 的 日 常 生 活

1 What are you doing?

兰兰在做什么？

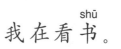

我在看^{shū}书。

我在听^{tīng yīnyuè}音乐。

我在写^{xiě zì}字。

我在喝^{chá}茶。

我在跳^{tiàowǔ}舞。

2 What time is it?

❸ What is your daily routine?

zǎoshang　qǐchuáng
你早上几点起床？

qǐchuáng
我七点起床。

zǎofàn
你几点吃早饭？

我七点半吃早饭。

shàngwǔ
你上午几点上学？

我八点二十分上学。

zhōngwǔ　　wǔfàn
你中午几点吃 午饭？

我十二点四十分吃午饭。

xiàwǔ　　fàngxué
你下午几点放学？

fàngxué
我三点放学。

wǎnfàn
你几点吃晚饭？

我六点半吃晚饭。

wǎnshang　　shuìjiào
你晚上几点睡觉？

kè　shuìjiào
我十点一刻睡觉。

4 You are late.

今天兰兰、大伟和小明去看九点的^{diànyǐng}电影。

小明^{lái}来了。

小明，你^{chídào}迟到了。

我^{chídào}迟到了？现在几点？
现在^{chà}差五分九点。

现在不是^{chà}差五分九点。现在是
九点十分。你的^{biǎo màn}表慢了。

^ò哦！^{zāogāo}糟糕，我的表慢了十五分。

^{yí}咦！你看，现在是九点五分。
大伟，你的^{biǎo kuài}表快了。

^{Zhēn de ma}真的吗？^ò哦！我的表快了五分。

好了！好了！我们^{yǐjīng}已经^{chídào}迟到了。
^{kuài}快^{jìnqu}进去吧！

 **Learn the sentences**

✳ Finding out what someone is doing

To ask What are you doing? say 你在做什么？ Nǐ zài zuò shénme? To be more informal say 你在干什么？ Nǐ zài gàn shénme? To answer, replace 什么 shénme with the activity. The word 在 zài, which is followed by a verb, shows that the person you are asking is still doing the activity.

你在做什么？	我在看书。 kàn shū
你在干什么？ gàn	我在看小人儿书。
她在做什么？	她在听音乐。 tīng yīnyuè
他在做什么？	他在做功课。 gōngkè
他们在干什么？ gàn	他们在下棋。 xiàqí

✳ Asking the time

To ask What's the time? say 现在几点？ Xiànzài jǐ diǎn? To state the time, start with the hour 点 diǎn, followed by the minute 分 fēn; finally, the second 秒 miǎo may also be included. Once again, the concept of big to small is seen here. Expressions such as a quarter past and a quarter to can also be used. To say a quarter past five, say 五点一刻 wǔ diǎn yí kè and to say a quarter to six, say 差一刻六点 chà yí kè liù diǎn. However, it is more common to say 15 minutes past, 十五分 shíwǔ fēn and 45 minutes past, 四十五分 sìshíwǔ fēn

现在几点？	现在三点。
现在几点？	现在七点十分。
现在几点？	现在八点一刻。 kè

现在几点？	九点半。
现在几点？	十点四十五分。
现在几点？	^{chà} 差五分十一点。
几点了？	^{kuài} 快十二点了。

✳ Asking what time someone does something

To ask What time do you get up? say 你几点起床？ Nǐ jǐ diǎn qǐchuáng? To answer, replace 几点 jǐ diǎn with the time. This pattern can be used to ask about many activities.

^{qǐchuáng} 你几点起床？	^{bàn qǐchuáng} 我七点半起床。
你几点上学？	我八点上学。
^{fàngxué} 你几点放学？	^{kè} 三点一刻。
^{shuìjiào} 你几点睡觉？	^{shuìjiào} 我九点四十五分睡觉。

To add in the morning or in the afternoon, the phrases 早上 zǎoshang- early morning, 上午 shàngwǔ- morning, 中午 zhōngwǔ- midday, 下午 xiàwǔ- afternoon and 晚上 wǎnshang evening should be placed before the time.

^{qǐchuáng} 你早上几点起床？	^{qǐchuáng} 我早上七点起床。
你上午几点上学？	我八点半上学。
你中午几点吃午饭？	我十二点十分吃午饭。
^{fàngxué} 你下午几点放学？	^{fàngxué} 三点半放学。
^{shuìjiào} 你晚上几点睡觉？	十一点。

✳ **Use of 了 le**

了 le, which has no English equivalent, has many uses and can be used after a verb, an adjective or at the end of a sentence.

To confirm or emphasize a situation:	tài 太好了！
To indicate a change in a situation:	我不吃了。 zhīdao 我知道了。 ná kuàizi 我会拿筷子了。 tóufa cháng 她的头发长了。
To indicate that the time is late:	现在几点了？ 十点半了。 kuài 快十二点了。 chídào 我快迟到了。
To urge someone to do something or to stop someone from doing something:	gāi 该你了。 qǐchuáng 该起床了。 好了！好了！
To emphasize that something happened in the past or to indicate that something has been completed:	lái 他来了。 我吃了。 qǐchuáng 他起床了。 biǎo màn 我的表慢了。

New words and expressions

日常	rìcháng	day-to-day, daily rì- day; cháng- usually, often
生活	shēnghuó	life shēng- birth, life; huó- to live, alive
在	zài	[indicates an action in progress]; at, in, on
做	zuò	to do, to make
功课	gōngkè	schoolwork, homework
		gōng- effort, merit; kè- lesson, subject
放	fàng	to let off, to let go, to release
风筝	fēngzhēng	kite fēng- wind; zhēng- a Chinese string instrument
干	gàn	to do, to work
下棋	xiàqí	to play chess
看	kàn	to read, to see, to watch, to look at
小人儿书	xiǎorénrshū	[oral] children's picture-story book
		xiǎo- little, small; rén- person; shū- book
写	xiě	to write
字	zì	character, word
听	tīng	to listen, to hear
音乐	yīnyuè	music yīn- sound; yuè- music
喝茶	hē chá	to have tea hē- to drink; chá- tea
跳舞	tiàowǔ	to dance tiào- to jump, to leap; wǔ- dance
现在	xiànzài	now, at present xiàn- now, present; zài- at
点	diǎn	o'clock; dot
分	fēn	minute
半	bàn	half
快	kuài	nearly; fast; hurry
该	gāi	should
进去	jìnqu	to go in, to enter jìn- to enter; qù- to go
早上	zǎoshang	(early) morning zǎo- morning, early; shang- [used after the noun to indicate scope]
起床	qǐchuáng	to get up, to get out of bed qǐ- to rise; chuáng- bed
早饭	zǎofàn	breakfast zǎo- early; fàn- meal, cooked rice
上午	shàngwǔ	morning shàng- first part, up; wǔ- noon, midday
中午	zhōngwǔ	midday, noon zhōng- middle; wǔ- noon, midday

午饭	wǔfàn	lunch wǔ- noon, midday; fàn- meal, cooked rice
下午	xiàwǔ	afternoon xià- latter part, under; wǔ- noon, midday
放学	fàngxué	to finish classes fàng- to let go, to release; xué- to study
晚饭	wǎnfàn	dinner wǎn- late; fàn- meal, cooked rice
晚上	wǎnshang	evening, night wǎn- evening, late; shang- [used after the noun to indicate scope]
睡觉	shuìjiào	to sleep shuì- to sleep; jiào- sleep
刻	kè	a quarter (of an hour)
电影	diànyǐng	movie diàn- electricity; yǐng- shadow, image
迟到	chídào	to arrive late chí- late; dào- to arrive
差	chà	differ from
表	biǎo	watch (timepiece)
慢	màn	slow; slowly
糟糕	zāogāo	[oral] oh no; how terrible zāo- in a wretched state; gāo- cake
已经	yǐjīng	already
零	líng	zero (in written form)

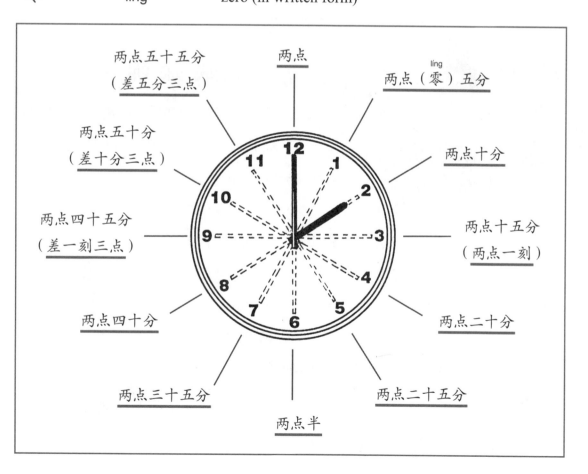

Write the characters

在	做	看	书	写
zài	zuò	kàn	shū	xiě
[in progress]; at, in, on	to do, to make	to read, see, watch	book	to write
字	现	点	分	半
zì	xiàn	diǎn	fēn	bàn
character, word	now, present	o'clock; dot	minute	half
了	下	午	早	晚
le	xià	wǔ	zǎo	wǎn
[grammatical word]	latter part; under	noon, midday	morning, early	evening, late

妹 妹 呢？

王利和他妹妹都^{dōu}喜欢宠物。王利

有一只大狗和两只小鸟^{niǎo}。他妹妹有一

只小猫^{māo}和五条^{tiáo}金鱼^{jīnyú}。

今天是星期天。

早上王利五点半起床^{qǐchuáng}，

五点三十五分去跑步^{pǎobù}，七点吃早饭，七点半和

爸爸下棋^{xiàqí}。现在是九点一刻^{kè}，王利在

看小人儿书^{xiǎorénrshū}，他爸爸在喝茶^{hēchá}，他妈妈

在听音乐^{tīng yīnyuè}。王利的妹妹呢^{ne}？她在做

什么？

Something to know

❀ Chinese tea

Tea is important in the daily life of the Chinese people. Tea contains caffeine, pigmentation, aromatic oils, vitamins, minerals and protein. People drink tea both at home and at work to quench their thirst, to refresh themselves and to aid digestion. Tea is also used as a medicine, in cooking and as a sacrificial offering. There are many varieties, which can generally be divided into three categories according to the method of manufacture: green tea, black tea and wulong tea. Green tea is unfermented; black tea is fully fermented and wulong tea is half fermented. There is also flower-scented tea with jasmine tea being the most popular. Every type of tea has its own characteristics.

There are two ways in which the Chinese enjoy tea: one is drinking, and the other is tasting. Weaker tea is drunk for refreshment and to quench the thirst. Strong tea is for tasting. The tea set for tasting consists of a small tray shaped like a shallow bowl, a small tea pot and four small cups. Each tea cup holds around 15 to 20 ml of tea, and the teapot makes just enough to fill the four cups. The tray is filled with hot water after the tea is made so as to keep the tea warm. In order to savour the quality, people drink tea slowly and with appreciation.

❀ Traditional leisure activities

Some Chinese children's games such as rope skipping, shuttlecock kicking, kite flying and top spinning have a long history. Chinese chess, xiàngqí 象棋, the "go" game, wéiqí 围棋, and mahjong, májiàng 麻将, are also popular leisure activities. Xiàngqí and wéiqí are both games for two people. The aim of xiàngqí is to take the opposition's general, and the aim of wéiqí is to encircle more territory than that held by the opposition. Májiàng is played by four people and is popular among those who have plenty of leisure time. Because playing májiàng is very time-consuming, somewhat engrossing and sometimes used for gambling, some people object to it.

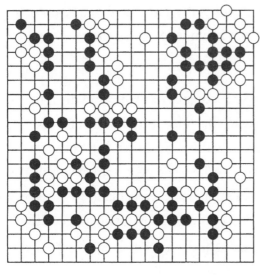

wéiqí 围棋

xiàngqí 象棋

❀ Daily routine of Chinese students

In China, students arrive at school early. Teams of students take turns sweeping up the leaves on the school grounds early in the morning. In high school, zhōngxué 中学, students still have most of the lessons in their homeroom as in elementary school. There are around 50 students in each class. The duration of the lesson is normally 45 minutes each with a 10-minute recess in between. Group physical exercise, which is normally held in the morning, is a daily routine. At some schools, eye exercises are also held each day to relax the eye muscles. At lunchtime, most of the students go home to have lunch. In Taiwan, students do not leave school during the lunch break, but take a short nap at their desks to refresh themselves for the afternoon lessons.

Apart from their curriculum subjects, students can choose to attend extracurricular activities, which may be held one or two afternoons each week. After cleaning the classroom at the end of the day, some students make their way home and some head for the Children's Palace, Shàoniángōng 少年宫. Children's Palaces are found in most cities in China to provide gifted students aged between seven and seventeen with specialized training in arts, science or sports.

dì　sān　kè　　Xiǎomíng　de　jiā
第三课 小明的家

1 Where are they?

　　小明家有六个人。他有爸爸、妈妈、一个哥哥、
一个姐姐和一个弟弟。他家还有一只小猫和一只小
狗。现在他们都在哪儿？

　　弟弟在车上面；爸爸在车下面。妈妈在车前面；
小明在车后面。姐姐在车右边；哥哥在车左边。小
狗在车里面；小猫在车外面。

2 House plan

这是小明的家。小明的家在兰兰家对面。兰兰
家是公寓。小明家是洋房。小明家前面是花园，后
面有一个游泳池。房子左边是阳台，下面是车库。

Dream home!

jiān wòshì　　　　　jiān shūfáng　　　kètīng
小明家有两间卧室、一间书房、一间客厅和一间

fàntīng　lìngwài hái　chúfáng　xǐyīfáng　cèsuǒ　yùshì　kètīng
饭厅。另外还有厨房、洗衣房、厕所和浴室。客厅在

zuì　　fàntīng　kètīng　　　　wòshì　kètīng　　　shūfáng
最前面。饭厅在客厅后面。两间卧室在客厅右边。书房

wòshì　　　　xǐyīfáng　cèsuǒ　yùshì　zuì
在卧室后面。洗衣房、厕所和浴室在最后面。

3 What happened?

妈，我回来了。

放学了？

是啊！都快四点了。

咦！怎么回事？
我们的沙发不见了。

沙发太旧了，我们买了
一套新的，明天送来。

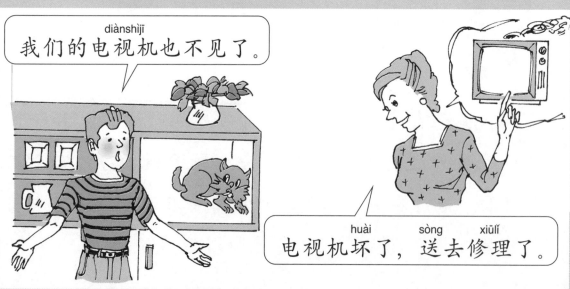

我们的电视机也不见了。

电视机坏了，送去修理了。

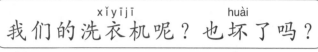

我们的洗衣机呢？也坏了吗？

是啊！洗衣机、电冰箱都坏了。

天哪！这是怎么回事？

糟糕！你的水床也破了。

真倒霉！我今天晚上睡哪儿？

唉！睡客厅地板吧！

4 Xiaoming's Sunday

今天是星期日。小明今天很早起床，很晚睡觉。
qǐchuáng shuìjiào

早上五点，他在游泳池游泳。
yóuyǒng chí

上午十点半，他在客厅沙发上睡觉。
kètīng shāfā shuìjiào

中午十二点，他在厨房打太极拳。
chúfáng tàijíquán

下午两点，他在洗衣房唱歌。
xǐyīfáng chànggē

下午六点，他在浴室里打电话。
yùshì diànhuà

晚上七点，他在电视机前面吃饭。
diànshìjī

晚上九点，他在书房看小人儿书。
shūfáng

半夜十二点，他在客厅做功课。
bànyè kètīng gōngkè

Learn the sentences

✳ **Asking the location of something**

To state a location, for example on top of the car, say 在车上面 zài chē shàngmian. In this example, the word 上面 shàngmian, indicating the location, should follow the object 车 chē to which it relates. The word order is the opposite of the English example.

chē 在车上面	在车下面
diànbīngxiāng 在电冰箱前面	在电冰箱后面
diànshìjī 在电视机左边	在电视机右边
chēkù 在车库里面	在车库外面

To state the location of someone or something, for example My shoes are on top of the car, say 我的鞋在车上面。Wǒ de xié zài chē shàngmian. To change this sentence into a question, replace the location 车上面 chē shàngmian with the question word 哪儿 nǎr or 哪里 nǎli. The sentence becomes 我的鞋在哪儿？Wǒ de xié zài nǎr? or 我的鞋在哪里？Wǒ de xié zài nǎli?

xié 我的鞋在哪儿？	chē 你的鞋在车上面。
我的书在哪儿？	shāfā 你的书在沙发下面。
shūfáng 你的书房在哪儿？	kètīng 在客厅后面。
cèsuǒ　　nǎli 你们的厕所在哪里？	zuì 在最后面。
nǎli 小明在哪里？	wòshì 他在卧室。
大伟，你在哪儿？	chúfáng 我在厨房。

In spoken Chinese, we can use 呢 ne instead of 在哪里 zài nǎli or 在哪儿 zài nǎr to ask where someone or something is.

我的鞋呢？ *xié ne*	在电冰箱上面！ *diànbīngxiāng*
我的书呢？ *ne*	我怎么知道？ *zhīdao*
我们的电视机呢？ *diànshìjī*	坏了，送去修理了。 *huài　sòng　xiūlǐ*

✳ Asking what someone is doing somewhere

In Lesson 2, we learnt how to ask what someone is doing. For example, the question 他在做什么？ Tā zài zuò shénme? and the reply 他在看电视。Tā zài kàn diànshì. To add the somewhere, place the location of the activity before the verb. To say He is watching TV in the living room, say 他在客厅看电视。Tā zài kètīng kàn diànshì.

他在客厅做什么？ *kètīng*	他在客厅看电视。 *kètīng　diànshì*
他在书房做什么？ *shūfáng*	他在书房做功课。 *shūfáng　gōngkè*
你在饭厅做什么？ *fàntīng*	吃饭。

✳ Asking where someone is doing something

To ask where someone is doing something, use the previous pattern but replace the location with the question word 哪儿 nǎr or 哪里 nǎli. The sentence 他在客厅看电视。Tā zài kètīng kàn diànshì. becomes 他在哪儿看电视？ Tā zài nǎr kàn diànshì? or 他在哪里看电视？ Tā zài nǎli kàn diànshì?

他在哪儿看电视？ *diànshì*	他在客厅看电视。 *kètīng　diànshì*
他在哪里睡觉？ *shuìjiào*	他在沙发上睡觉。 *shāfā　shuìjiào*
他在哪儿吃饭？	他在电视机前面吃饭。 *diànshìjī*

✳ **Asking what happened**

To ask What happened? or What's the matter? say 怎么回事？Zěnme huí shì? Here, 回 huí is a measure word for 事 shì.

怎么回事？	我们的电视机坏了。 diànshìjī huài
这是怎么回事？	我们的车坏了。 chē huài
这是怎么回事？	你的水床破了。 shuǐchuáng pò

✳ **Finding out where someone sleeps**

We have learnt that to ask Where do I sleep? 我在哪儿睡觉？Wǒ zài nǎr shuìjiào? which is a formal expression. In spoken Chinese, it is more common to say 我睡哪儿？Wǒ shuì nǎr?

你昨天晚上睡哪儿？ shuì	睡客厅地板。 shuì kètīng dìbǎn
你今天晚上睡哪儿？	睡我弟弟的 床。 chuáng
你明天晚上睡哪儿？	睡客厅沙发。 kètīng shāfā

New words and expressions

在	zài	at, in, on; [indicating an action in progress]
哪儿	nǎr	[oral] where, also said as 哪里 nǎli nǎ- where, which, what; (é)r- [a word ending]
车	chē	car, vehicle
上面	shàngmian	on top of, above shàng- up, above; miàn- [word ending - location], face
下面	xiàmian	under, below xià- down, under
前面	qiánmian	front qián- front, before
后面	hòumian	behind hòu- behind, after
左边	zuǒbian	left (location) zuǒ- left; biān- [word ending - location], side
右边	yòubian	right (location) yòu- right
里面	lǐmian	inside lǐ- inside
外面	wàimian	outside wài- outside
对面	duìmian	opposite (location) duì- opposite, correct
公寓	gōngyù	flats, units, apartment; (multi-storey building – 楼房 lóufáng)
洋房	yángfáng	Western-style house; (single-storey house – 平房 píngfáng) yáng- foreign, ocean; fáng- house; píng- flat, level
花园	huāyuán	garden huā- flower; yuán- garden, park
游泳池	yóuyǒng chí	swimming pool yóuyǒng- to swim; chí- pool, pond
房子	fángzi	house
阳台	yángtái	balcony, veranda yáng- the sun; tái- platform
车库	chēkù	garage chē- vehicle; kù- storehouse, storage
间	jiān	[a measure word for room]
卧室	wòshì	bedroom wò- to lie down; shì- room
书房	shūfáng	study shū- book; fáng- room, house
客厅	kètīng	living room kè- guest; tīng- hall
饭厅	fàntīng	dining room fàn- meal, cooked rice; tīng- hall
另外	lìngwài	in addition, besides
还	hái	also, still
厨房	chúfáng	kitchen chú- kitchen; fáng- room, house
洗衣房	xǐyīfáng	laundry xǐ- to wash; yī- clothes; fáng- room, house
厕所	cèsuǒ	toilet, lavatory cè- toilet, lavatory; suǒ- place
浴室	yùshì	bathroom, shower room yù- to bathe; shì- room

最	zuì	most
回来	huílai	to come back, to return huí- to return; lái- to come
都	dōu	already; all
怎么回事	zěnme huí shì	what happened; what's the matter zěnme- what, why; huí- [a measure word for matter]; shì- affair, matter
沙发	shāfā	sofa (transliteration of sofa)
见	jiàn	to see, to catch sight of
太	tài	too (exceedingly)
旧	jiù	old (nonliving things), worn
套	tào	[a measure word for clothing or furniture], set, suit
新	xīn	new
送	sòng	to deliver, to send
送来	sòng lái	to deliver or send to (here) lái- to come
电视机	diànshìjī	television set diànshì- television; jī- machine
坏	huài	broken down; bad
送去	sòng qù	to deliver or send to (there) qù- to go
修理	xiūlǐ	to repair, to fix xiū- to repair; lǐ- to put in order
洗衣机	xǐyījī	washing machine xǐ- to wash; yī- clothes; jī- machine
电冰箱	diànbīngxiāng	refrigerator diàn- electricity; bīng- ice; xiāng- box
天哪	tiān na	Good heavens! tiān- sky, heaven; na- [a word ending]
水床	shuǐchuáng	water bed shuǐ- water; chuáng- bed
破	pò	broken, torn
倒霉	dǎoméi	to have bad luck dǎo- upside down; méi- mould
睡	shuì	to sleep
唉	ài	(a sigh)
地板	dìbǎn	floor dì- floor, ground; bǎn- board
早	zǎo	early
晚	wǎn	late
打	dǎ	to play (ball game, taichi etc); to dial (telephone)
太极拳	tàijíquán	taichi
唱歌	chànggē	to sing, singing chàng- to sing; gē- song
电话	diànhuà	telephone diàn- electricity; huà- speech
电视	diànshì	television diàn- electricity; shì- to look at, sight
半夜	bànyè	midnight bàn- half; yè- night, evening
鞋	xié	shoes

háiyǒu = also has

xǐ zǎo jiān = shower room

less formal than

yùshì

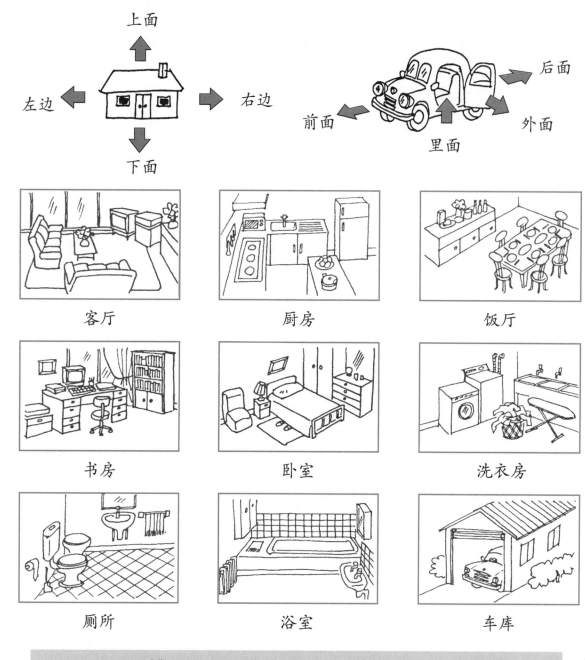

上面

左边　　右边

下面

后面

前面　　外面

里面

客厅　　厨房　　饭厅

书房　　卧室　　洗衣房

厕所　　浴室　　车库

【小谜语】 (míyǔ)

1. 两个人，不是从(cóng)。（猜(cāi)一字）

2. 生日。（猜(cāi)一字）

3. 九天加(jiā)一天。（猜(cāi)一字）

4. 家里没有动物，也没有大人。（猜(cāi)一字）

Write the characters

哪 nǎ where; which; what	儿 ér [word ending]	前 qián front, before	面 miàn [word ending]; face	后 hòu behind, after
右 yòu right (location)	边 biān [word ending]; side	左 zuǒ left (location)	里 lǐ inside	外 wài outside
回 huí to return; [measure word]	来 lái to come	怎 zěn how	事 shì matter, business	见 jiàn to see

家

　　王利的家很大，前面是游泳池(yóuyǒng chí)，后面有一个大花园(huāyuán)。王利的卧室(wòshì)在左边最(zuì)后面，浴室(yùshì)和厕所(cèsuǒ)在他房间(fángjiān)右边。

　　今天晚上，王利一家人七点半吃晚饭。他爸爸在车库(chēkù)里吃，妈妈在厨房(chúfáng)里吃，妹妹在卧室(wòshì)里吃，王利在书房(shūfáng)里吃。吃了晚饭，王利一家人都在客厅(kètīng)：王利在听音乐(tīng yīnyuè)，妹妹在唱歌(chànggē)，爸爸在看电视(diànshì)，妈妈在看书。

Something to know

❀ Housing

Because of the high population density, the traditional U-shaped Chinese house, called sìhéyuàn 四合院, has almost disappeared except for a few places in the country. The U-shaped house, surrounding a court yard, was usually made of mud bricks, with some luxurious ones being built of clay bricks. The room in which ancestors were worshipped was in the centre of the house. More rooms could be added behind the two wings of the U-shaped building, which made it an ideal house for the traditionally large family consisting of grandparents, aunts and uncles, parents, children and grandchildren. In the 20th century, because of the emergence of the nuclear family, apartments have become the main form of housing, especially in urban areas.

In the city in China, housing is traditionally provided by government employers, called dānwèi 单位. Workers lease their units from their dānwèi for a very low rent. The unit usually contains small rooms and the toilet is often shared by a few families. To save room, people often use the little veranda for cooking as well as for drying clothes. There are units containing better facilities for more affluent people, but they are not numerous. In recent years, a private housing policy has been introduced, and people are being encouraged to buy their own units.

In the country, many families still have three generations living together, that is, grandparents, parents and children. After 1978, the commune system was dismantled, and agricultural production returned to being based on the family unit. A "free market" was established for farmers to earn extra money from selling surplus grain, fruit, vegetables and chickens. Some peasants have become wealthy compared to those who live in the city and earn a salary. They can afford to build their own houses or even two- or three-storey mansions equipped with better and more modern electrical facilities.

In Taiwan, the standard of living is similar to that of the West. Due to the high population density and the scarcity of land, people in the cities mainly live in high-rise buildings. However, there are still traditional U-shaped houses in country areas, although they are also disappearing, to be replaced with multi-storey buildings.

sìhéyuàn 四合院

dì sì kè wǒ de yīfu
第四课 我的衣服

1 What clothes do they wear?

chuān　　yīfu
他们穿什么衣服？

Wáng xiānsheng chuān hēisè   xīzhuāng
王先生穿黑色的西装。
tàitai   lǜsè   liányīqún
王太太穿绿色的连衣裙。

Lǐ   bái chènshān lán kùzi
李老师穿白衬衫、蓝裤子。
Bái   zǐ qípáo
白小姐穿紫旗袍。

hóng mián'ǎo
小妹妹穿红棉袄。
hànshān
小弟弟穿白色的汗衫、
kāfēisè   duǎnkù
咖啡色的短裤。

qiǎn huángsè   máoyī
兰兰穿浅黄色的毛衣、
shēn   qúnzi   chéngsè
深黄色的裙子和橙色
wàitào
的外套。

2 Do they fit?

jiàn chènshān cháng
这件衬衫太长了；

duǎn
那件衬衫太短了。

tiáo qúnzi féi
这条裙子太肥了；

shòu
那条裙子太瘦了。

tào xīzhuāng
这套西装太大了；

那套西装太小了。

qípáo qǐlai héshēn
这件旗袍穿起来很合身。

hànshān qǐlai shūfu
那件汗衫穿起来很舒服。

mián'ǎo shímáo
这件棉袄看起来很时髦。

tiáo liányīqún piàoliang
那条连衣裙看起来很漂亮。

3 **What should I wear?**

妈，今天是小明的生日。
我该(gāi)穿哪件衣服呢(ne)？

穿那条(tiáo)绿色的连衣裙(liányīqún)吧！

那条连衣裙太瘦(shòu)了，不好看。

那么，那条蓝色的呢？

那条太长(cháng)了。我不喜欢。

妈，你看这件红衬衫(chènshān)配(pèi)这条黑裙子(qúnzi)怎么样(zěnmeyàng)？

啊(a)！挺(tǐng)时髦(shímáo)，挺(tǐng)好看的。

4 **Where are my shoes?**

唉！我那 双 黑色的新皮鞋呢？

哥，我的新皮鞋在哪儿？

我怎么知道？自己找找。

姐，你有没有看到我的新皮鞋？

没有。浴室里找找吧！

不在浴室。妈！你有没有看到我的皮鞋？

好像在厨房冰箱旁边。

不是这双。这双是旧的。
我在找新的。

新的？客厅里找找吧！

找到了。在电视机上面。

小明，看看你的袜子，一只
是白的，一只是黑的。

哦……时髦嘛！

48

Learn the sentences

✲ **Asking what someone is wearing**

To ask what clothes someone is wearing, use 穿什么衣服 chuān shénme yīfu. This is often shortened to 穿什么 chuān shénme. To answer, replace this phrase with a description of the clothes being worn.

他今天穿什么衣服？	他穿黄<ruby>衬衫<rt>chènshān</rt></ruby>、黑<ruby>裤子<rt>kùzi</rt></ruby>。
她今天穿什么？	她穿蓝<ruby>旗袍<rt>qípáo</rt></ruby>。
她昨天穿什么？	她穿绿色的<ruby>连衣裙<rt>liányīqún</rt></ruby>。

✲ **Describing how clothes fit**

When describing something using 太 tài- too, 了 le is usually used after the stative verb. For example, to say too big, say 太大了 tài dà le. However, to use phrases such as not too, the 了 le is not used. Therefore, to say not too big, say 不太大 bú tài dà.

这 <ruby>双<rt>shuāng</rt></ruby> <ruby>皮鞋<rt>píxié</rt></ruby> 太大了。	那双皮鞋太小了。
这 <ruby>条<rt>tiáo</rt></ruby> <ruby>裙子<rt>qúnzi</rt></ruby> 太<ruby>肥<rt>féi</rt></ruby>了。	那条裙子太<ruby>瘦<rt>shòu</rt></ruby>了。
我的 <ruby>裤子<rt>kùzi</rt></ruby> 太<ruby>长<rt>cháng</rt></ruby>了。	你的裤子太<ruby>短<rt>duǎn</rt></ruby>了。
这件衣服不太大。	那件<ruby>毛衣<rt>máoyī</rt></ruby>不太小。

✲ **Use of** 起来 qǐlai **after the verb**

The meaning of 起来 qǐlai is literally to stand up, to rise. However, it can be used after a verb to express an impression or an opinion of something.

那件衣服她穿<ruby>起来<rt>qǐlái</rt></ruby>很<ruby>合身<rt>héshēn</rt></ruby>。

这件衣服穿起来真不<ruby>舒服<rt>shūfu</rt></ruby>。

你的<ruby>棉袄<rt>mián'ǎo</rt></ruby>看起来很<ruby>漂亮<rt>piàoliang</rt></ruby>。

她的<ruby>连衣裙<rt>liányīqún</rt></ruby>看起来很<ruby>时髦<rt>shímáo</rt></ruby>。

这个<ruby>汉堡包<rt>hànbǎobāo</rt></ruby>看起来不好看，吃起来很好吃。

✳ Wondering what to wear

To ask Which clothes should I wear? say 我该穿哪件衣服呢？Wǒ gāi chuān nǎ jiàn yīfu ne? Here, 该 gāi means should.

我明天<ruby>该<rt>gāi</rt></ruby>穿哪件衣服呢？

我今天该穿哪件衣服呢？

我明天该穿哪<ruby>双<rt>shuāng</rt></ruby> <ruby>皮鞋<rt>píxié</rt></ruby>呢？

穿那件<ruby>紫<rt>zǐ</rt></ruby><ruby>旗袍<rt>qípáo</rt></ruby>吧！

穿那<ruby>套<rt>tào</rt></ruby>蓝色的<ruby>西装<rt>xīzhuāng</rt></ruby>吧！

穿那双黑色的吧！

✳ Asking for an opinion

To ask an opinion from someone on something, use 怎么样 zěnmeyàng, which means how about or what about. To say How about this? or What about this? say 这个怎么样？Zhè gè zěnmeyàng?

这个怎么样？

这件衣服怎么样？

那<ruby>双<rt>shuāng</rt></ruby> <ruby>皮鞋<rt>píxié</rt></ruby>怎么样？

这<ruby>条<rt>tiáo</rt></ruby> <ruby>裙子<rt>qúnzi</rt></ruby>怎么样？

<ruby>挺<rt>tǐng</rt></ruby>好的。

<ruby>挺<rt>tǐng</rt></ruby>好看的。

穿<ruby>起来<rt>qǐlái</rt></ruby><ruby>挺<rt>tǐng</rt></ruby><ruby>舒服<rt>shūfu</rt></ruby>的。

太<ruby>肥<rt>féi</rt></ruby>了。

The verb 看 kàn, literally meaning to see, can be used to ask an opinion and is equivalent to to think. Therefore, 你看怎么样？Nǐ kàn zěnmeyàng? means What do you think?

mián'ǎo 你看这件棉袄怎么样？ chènshān 你看这件衬衫怎么样？	tǐng piàoliang 挺漂亮的。 我看太大了。

✳ **Use of** 有没有 yǒu méi yǒu **before a verb**

We have learnt to use 有没有 yǒu méi yǒu to ask whether someone has something, i.e. 你有没有哥哥？Nǐ yǒu méi yǒu gēge? In this situation, 有没有 yǒu méi yǒu is used before a noun. It can also be used before a verb to indicate an inquiry as to whether something has happened in the past. This usage is particularly common in Taiwan. To say Did you have breakfast? say 你有没有吃早饭？Nǐ yǒu méi yǒu chī zǎofàn?

kàndào　　xié 你有没有看到我的鞋？ 你今天有没有吃早饭？ yóuyǒng 你昨天有没有去游泳？	shāfā 有，在沙发下面。 没有。 我没有去。

*People wearing the traditional clothing chángpáo mǎguà 长袍马褂
acting the comic dialogue xiàngshēng 相声*

New words and expressions

衣服	yīfu	clothes, clothing yī- clothes; fú- clothes
穿	chuān	to wear (clothes, shoes or socks)
王	Wáng	a surname wáng- king
先生	xiānsheng	Mr.; (in Taiwan) husband xiān- first; shēng- born
黑色	hēisè	black hēi- black; sè- colour
西装	xīzhuāng	Western-style attire, suit xī- west; zhuāng- outfit
太太	tàitai	Mrs.; (in Taiwan) wife tài- too
绿色	lǜsè	green lǜ- green; sè- colour
连衣裙	liányīqún	woman's dress, called 洋装 yángzhuāng in Taiwan lián- to join; yī- clothes; qún- skirt; yáng- foreign; zhuāng- outfit
白	bái	white
衬衫	chènshān	shirt
蓝	lán	blue
裤子	kùzi	trousers, pants
小姐	xiǎojie	Miss.; young lady
紫	zǐ	purple
旗袍	qípáo	a close-fitting dress with a high neck and a slit skirt
红	hóng	red
棉袄	mián'ǎo	cotton-padded coat
白色	báisè	white bái- white; sè- colour
汗衫	hànshān	undershirt, T-shirt hàn- sweat; shān- shirt
咖啡色	kāfēisè	brown kāfēi- (transliteration of coffee); sè- colour
短裤	duǎnkù	shorts duǎn- short; kù- pants, trousers
浅	qiǎn	light (colour); shallow
黄色	huángsè	yellow huáng- yellow; sè- colour
毛衣	máoyī	sweater máo- fur, feather; yī- clothes
深	shēn	dark (colour); deep
裙子	qúnzi	skirt
橙色	chéngsè	orange (colour) chéng- orange; sè- colour
外套	wàitào	coat wài- outside; tào- cover
件	jiàn	[a measure word for clothing or affair]
条	tiáo	[a measure word for trousers, skirt, river, belt etc.]
肥	féi	loose-fitting (clothing), (宽 kuān is used in Taiwan); fat
瘦	shòu	tight-fitting (clothing), (窄 zhǎi is used in Taiwan); thin

穿起来	chuān qǐlai	impression or feeling of the clothes on someone
合身	héshēn	well-fitting (clothing)　hé- fit; shēn- body
舒服	shūfu	comfortable　shū- comfortable; fú- comfortable, clothes
看起来	kàn qǐlai	looks, impression or feeling of the look
时髦	shímáo	fashion, fashionable
漂亮	piàoliang	pretty　piào- pretty; liàng- bright, shinning
配	pèi	to match
怎么样	zěnmeyàng	how about, what about　zěnme- how, what; yàng- appearance
挺	tǐng	[oral] very
好看	hǎokàn	good-looking
双	shuāng	[a measure word for shoes, socks, gloves etc.] pair
皮鞋	píxié	leather shoes　pí- leather; xié- shoes
怎么	zěnme	how, what
自己	zìjǐ	self
找找	zhǎozhao	to have a look for　zhǎo- to look for
看到	kàndào	to catch sight of, to see　kàn- to see; dào- to reach
好像	hǎoxiàng	seem, be like　hǎo- good; xiàng- alike
冰箱	bīngxiāng	refrigerator　bīng- ice; xiāng- box
旁边	pángbian	the side
找到了	zhǎodào le	found　zhǎo- to look for; dào- to reach, to arrive
看看	kànkan	to have a look　kàn- to see, to look
袜子	wàzi	socks
只	zhī	[a measure word for animal or single shoe and sock]
嘛	ma	[word ending, indicates an obvious situation]

Write the characters

穿	衣	服	先	太
chuān *to wear*	yī *clothes*	fú *clothes*	xiān *first*	tài *too (exceedingly)*
黑	白	红	黄	蓝
hēi *black*	bái *white*	hóng *red*	huáng *yellow*	lán *blue*
绿	色	件	呢	找
lù *green*	sè *colour*	jiàn *[measure word]*	ne *[question word]*	zhǎo *to look for*

太 时髦(shímáo) 了

王利的妹妹有很多衣服：衬衫(chènshān)、裙子(qúnzi)、毛衣(máoyī)、外套(wàitào)、连衣裙(liányīqún)；白色的，黑色的，红色的，黄色的，蓝色的，绿色的，很多很多。今天她不知道(zhīdao)该(gāi)穿哪件衣服，她说："这条(tiáo)太长(cháng)了，那条太短(duǎn)了……这件太肥(féi)了，那件太瘦(shòu)了……这条太旧(jiù)了，那条太新(xīn)了……这件太合身(héshēn)了，那件太时髦(shímáo)了……"

Something to know

✿ Traditional clothes today

Some clothing worn by the Chinese today still retains the Mandarin style of the Qing dynasty, but with some modifications. Qípáo 旗袍 and mián'ǎo 棉袄 are the two most popular styles. Qípáo is a close-fitting dress with a high neck and a slit skirt. It is still regarded as women's formal dress. Mián'ǎo is a cotton-padded jacket. The softness and warmth of the jacket makes it ideal for the cold winter. Chángpáo mǎguà 长袍马褂, a mandarin jacket worn over a gown by men, is no longer everyday wear but is worn on the stage, particularly by those who perform xiàngshēng 相声, a comic dialogue (see the drawing on page 50). The best material for this clothing is silk.

A style, in white, worn by Dr. Sun Yat-sen called Zhōngshānzhuāng 中山装, was once popular, and the style, in blue, worn by Nikolai Lenin called Lièníngzhuāng 列宁装 became popular in China after China became a communist country in 1949 and is still worn today by some people.

✿ Chinese silk

Silk cloth in China dates back to the Neolithic period, around 7,000 to 1,600 B.C.. Silk is produced from the cocoons of silkworms, which are raised on woven trays and fed with hand-picked mulberry leaves. Before the moths emerge, the cocoons are plunged into boiling water and the silk fibre is reeled off. With care, the fibre can be reeled off in a continuous unbroken thread to an average length of around 500 metres. The silk fibre is then used to produce a luxurious textile. Silk is light, soft, smooth and durable.

In the early days, silk was the favourite textile of the imperial family and was often used as gifts for rulers of other countries. The Silk Road, a route from China to overseas, was gradually formed due to the export of silk to Japan and to the West. Today, silk is still one of the main exports of China. The embroidery of Sūzhōu 苏州, called sūxiù 苏绣, and that of Húnán 湖南, called xiāngxiù 湘绣, are world famous.

✿ Chinese colours

Traditionally, Chinese regarded white as the colour of mourning and red as the colour of luck. Before the influence of the West and the popularity of the white wedding dress in the 20th century, Chinese brides wore red wedding dresses. Yellow is particularly associated with the emperor. The garment of the emperor was described as the *Yellow Robe*, Huángpáo 黄袍, which is normally decorated with the dragon. Gold, the colour of wealth, green, the colour of prosperity, and red were used for the decorations of the imperial palace and are still widely used in many Taoist temples in Taiwan.

dì wǔ kè mǎi dōngxi
第 五 课 买 东 西

1 How much is it?

	shuāng xié duōshǎo qián 这 双 鞋多少钱？	65.00	kuài 六十五块
	tiáo kùzi 这条裤子多少钱？	37.00	三十七块
	dǐng màozi 这顶帽子多少钱？	4.50	四块半
	tiáo liányīqún 这条连衣裙多少钱？	78.50	七十八块五
	xiāngjiāo　　　　jīn 香蕉多少钱一斤？	1.30	一块三
	júzi　　　　dài 橘子多少钱一袋？	3.80	三块八
	bōluó 菠萝多少钱一个？	1.05	líng 一块零五分
	cǎoméi　　　mài 草莓怎么卖？	2.85	máo　　jīn 两块八毛五一斤
	lìzhī 荔枝怎么卖？	1.49	一块四毛九一斤

2 In the department store

yào dào bǎihuò shāngdiàn mǎi dōngxi
小明今天要到百货商店买东西。
shūbāo huài　　　　　　xīn
他的书包坏了。他想买个新的。

qǐngwèn　　　　　　　　shūbāo
请问，你们这儿卖书包吗？

卖。这个好不好？

tǐng　　　　　　yào
挺好的，可是我不要绿色的。
有没有蓝色的？

zěnmeyàng
有。这个怎么样？

这个还不错。多少钱？

十三块五。

十三块五？太贵了。
有没有便宜点儿的？

这个便宜点儿，七块四。

好，我要这个。给你十块钱。

找您两块六。谢谢。

3 In the bookshop

shūdiàn　dōngxi
大伟今天到书店买东西。

qǐngwèn　　　　　　dìtú
请问，你们有中国地图吗？

duìbuqǐ　　　　　　dìtú
对不起，我们没有中国地图。

zìdiǎn
那你们有字典吗？

nín　　　zìdiǎn
有。您要什么字典？

běn Hàn-Yīng zìdiǎn
我要一本汉英字典。

Hàn-Yīng　zìdiǎn
这是汉英字典。

这本太大了。有没有小点儿的？

这本怎么样？

tǐng
挺好的。我买这本。我还
zázhì　　　　fèn　bàozhǐ
要一本杂志和一份报纸，
yígòng
一共多少钱？

zìdiǎn　　　　　　　zázhì
字典三块二，杂志六毛，
bàozhǐ
报纸三毛五，一共四块
一毛五。

这是四块一毛五。

谢谢。

4 At the market

王小姐今天到市场买水果。

小姐，买什么？

苹果甜不甜？怎么卖？

很甜。一斤一块四。

我买两斤。

这是两斤苹果。还要什么？

葡萄多少钱一斤？

三块六一斤。

Learn the sentences

✳ **Asking the price**

To ask how much (money), say 多少钱 duōshǎo qián. To state an amount of money, use the measure words 块 kuài for dollars, 毛 máo for ten-cent units and 分 fēn for cents from one to nine. In spoken Chinese, the last measure word 分 fēn is not normally said, but to avoid confusion, 分 must be said if there are no ten-cent units. For example, to say ¥5.30, say 五块三 wǔ kuài sān, to say ¥5.03, say 五块零三分 wǔ kuài líng sān fēn. When the amount of money ends in 50 cents, 半 bàn can be used to indicate half a dollar, or simply use 五.

这本字典多少钱？ zìdiǎn	两块。
这件衣服多少钱？	十五块七。
这顶帽子多少钱？ dǐng màozi	八块六毛九。
这 双 皮鞋多少钱？ shuāng píxié	七十五块半。

¥1.00: 一块/元　　　　¥0.10: 一毛/角　　　　¥0.01: 一分
      yuán　　　　　　　　　jiǎo

¥0.50: 五毛/角　　　　¥1.50: 一块半 or 一块五
      jiǎo

To ask the price of something by item, pairs or weight, place the measure word before or after 多少钱 duōshǎo qián. To ask How much each? say 一个多少钱？ Yí gè duōshǎo qián? or 多少钱一个？ Duōshǎo qián yí gè?

多少钱一斤？ jīn	一斤多少钱？
多少钱一个？	一个多少钱？
香蕉多少钱一斤？ xiāngjiāo　　jīn	香蕉一斤多少钱？
报纸多少钱一份？ bàozhǐ　　　fèn	报纸一份多少钱？ fèn
杂志多少钱一本？ zázhì	杂志一本多少钱？

Another way to ask about price is to use 怎么卖 zěnme mài, which means how is (it) sold. The reply may be ¥3.00 a bag 一袋三块 yí dài sān kuài or perhaps 50 cents each 一个五毛 yí gè wǔ máo.

píngguǒ 苹果怎么卖？	jīn 一斤一块三。
bōluó 菠萝怎么卖？	一个八毛。
júzi 橘子怎么卖？	dài 一袋两块五。

✳ **Asking if something is for sale**

To ask Do you sell school bags? say 你们卖书包吗？ Nǐmen mài shūbāo ma? The reply for yes is 卖 mài and for no 不卖 bú mài. Alternatively, ask Do you have school bags? 你们有书包吗？ Nǐmen yǒu shūbāo ma?

shūbāo 请问，你们卖书包吗？	卖。
zìdiǎn 请问，你们卖字典吗？	duìbuqǐ 对不起，我们不卖。
shūbāo 请问，你们有书包吗？	有。你要哪个？
dìtú 请问，你们有地图吗？	duìbuqǐ 对不起，我们没有。

✻ **Expressing an opinion on goods or asking for a choice**

_{mián'ǎo} _{guì}
这件棉袄还不错，可是太贵了。

_{chènshān tǐng}
这件衬衫挺好的，可是太大了。

_{guì} _{piányi}
这件毛衣太贵了，有没有便宜点儿的？

_{shuāng　píxié}
这 双 皮鞋太大了，有没有小点儿的？

_{pútao　suān} _{tián}
这葡萄太酸了，有没有甜点儿的？

我不要蓝色的，有没有绿色的？

✻ **Asking whether something is sweet or sour**

To ask whether something is sweet, use 甜不甜 tián bù tián; for sour, use 酸不酸 suān bù suān.

_{píngguǒ tián}
苹果甜不甜？　　　　很甜。

_{bōluó} _{fēicháng}
菠萝甜不甜？　　　　非常甜。

_{júzi　suān}
橘子酸不酸？　　　　不太酸。

_{pútao} _{dōu}
葡萄酸不酸？　　　　一点儿都不酸。

✻ **Stating degree**

extremely	very	not very	not	not at all
_{fēicháng tián} 非常甜	很甜	不太甜	不甜	_{dōu} 一点儿都不甜
_{suān} 非常酸	很酸	不太酸	不酸	一点儿都不酸

✳ **Use of 的 de**

1. 的 can be used after a noun, a pronoun, an adjective or a verb to form an attribute to modify the word that follows it. The word being modified can be omitted if it is previously mentioned or is obviously known.

after a noun/pronoun (possessive):	姐姐的书；姐姐的 我的衣服；我的
after a noun/pronoun (modifying):	红色的衬衫；红色的 chènshān 九点的电影；九点的 diànyǐng
after a conditional verb:	昨天买的苹果；昨天买的 píngguǒ 要去打球的人；要去打球的 一九八四年生的人；一九八四年生的
after an adjective:	红的衬衫；红的 chènshān 新的皮鞋；新的 píxié 便宜点儿的书包；便宜点儿的 piányi 小点儿的字典；小点儿的 zìdiǎn

(When the adjective is a single character, 的 is often omitted, e.g. 红衬衫, 新皮鞋)

2. 的 used in spoken form:

used after 挺:	挺好的，挺漂亮的 tǐng　　piàoliang
used for emphasis:	真的 (Really?/Really!)
used to soften a reply:	是—是的；好—好的

New words and expressions

多少	duōshǎo	how much, how many
		duō- many, much, more; shǎo- few, little, less
钱	qián	money
块	kuài	[oral] monetary unit for dollars, formally called 元 yuán
顶	dǐng	[a measure word for hat, cap]; top
帽子	màozi	hat, cap
香蕉	xiāngjiāo	banana xiāng- fragrant; jiāo- a broadleaf plant
斤	jīn	a unit of weight = 0.5 kilograms
橘子	júzi	mandarin, tangerine
袋	dài	bag
菠萝	bōluó	pineapple, also called 凤梨 fènglí
毛	máo	[oral] 10-cent unit (= 0.1 元 yuán), formally called 角 jiǎo
草莓	cǎoméi	strawberry cǎo- straw; méi- berry
卖	mài	to sell
荔枝	lìzhī	lychee
分	fēn	a unit of money, cent (= 0.01 元 yuán or 块 kuài)
百货商店	bǎihuò	department store bǎi- one hundred; huò- goods;
	shāngdiàn	shāng- business; diàn- shop
可是	kěshì	but, however
还不错	hái búcuò	[oral] not bad, pretty good bù- not; cuò- wrong
贵	guì	expensive, dear
便宜	piányi	cheap, inexpensive
点儿	diǎnr	a little diǎn- dot, o'clock; (é)r- [a word ending]
给	gěi	to give
找	zhǎo	to make change; to look for
您	nín	[polite form] you
书店	shūdiàn	bookshop shū- book; diàn- shop
地图	dìtú	map dì- ground; tú- picture
那	nà	[conjunction] then, shorten from 那么 nàme
字典	zìdiǎn	dictionary zì- word; diǎn- record, book
要	yào	to want; to be going to

本	běn	[a measure word for books, magazines and dictionaries]
汉英字典	Hàn-Yīng zìdiǎn	Chinese-English dictionary
		Hàn- China, name of a dynasty; Yīng- English
杂志	zázhì	magazine　zá- miscellaneous; zhì- record, annals
份	fèn	[a measure word for newspapers, copies], orally often
		said as fènr 份儿
报纸	bàozhǐ	newspaper　bào- to report; zhǐ - paper
一共	yígòng	all together　yī- one; gòng- together
市场	shìchǎng	market　shì- market; chǎng- place
水果	shuǐguǒ	fruit　shuǐ- water; guǒ- fruit
苹果	píngguǒ	apple
甜	tián	sweet
葡萄	pútao	grape
酸	suān	sour
一点儿都不	yìdiǎnr dōu bù	not at all...　yìdiǎnr- a little; dōu- all; bù- not
非常	fēicháng	extremely　fēi- not; cháng- usually, often
串	chuàn	[a measure word for grapes or bananas] bunch, cluster
元	yuán	[formal] monetary unit for dollar, also written as 圆
角	jiǎo	[formal] 10-cent unit

香蕉	橘子	菠萝	草莓
荔枝	苹果	葡萄	水果
地图	字典	杂志	报纸

✏️ Write the characters

多	少	钱	买	卖
duō	shǎo	qián	mǎi	mài
many, much, more	*few, little, less*	*money*	*to buy*	*to sell*
块	毛	到	样	还
kuài	máo	dào	yàng	hái
dollar	*10-cent unit*	*to arrive, to go to*	*appearance*	*also; still*
要	给	谢	本	共
yào	gěi	xiè	běn	gòng
to want; to be going to	*to give*	*to thank*	*[measure word]*	*together*

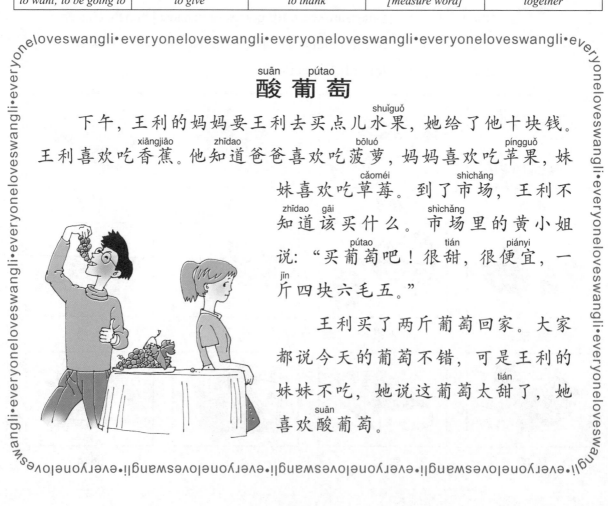

everyoneloveswangli•everyoneloveswangli•everyoneloveswangli•everyoneloveswangli•everyone

酸 葡 萄
suān　pútao

　　下午，王利的妈妈要王利去买点儿水果，她给了他十块钱。
王利喜欢吃香蕉。他知道爸爸喜欢吃菠萝，妈妈喜欢吃苹果，妹妹喜欢吃草莓。到了市场，王利不知道该买什么。市场里的黄小姐说："买葡萄吧！很甜，很便宜，一斤四块六毛五。"

　　王利买了两斤葡萄回家。大家都说今天的葡萄不错，可是王利的妹妹不吃，她说这葡萄太甜了，她喜欢酸葡萄。

Something to know

❀ The currencies in China and Taiwan

The currency used in China is called rénmínbì 人民币, *people's money*, and the monetary symbol is ¥. The currency used in Taiwan is called xīntáibì 新台币, *new currency of Taiwan,* and the monetary symbol is $. The numbers used on notes and coins are in a complicated form, i.e. 壹(一)、貳(二)、叁(三)、肆(四)、伍(五)、陆(六)、柒(七)、捌(八)、玖(九)、拾(十). Cheques are also written in this form so they cannot be easily altered. Commodity prices in China, although varying at times, are generally much lower than in Australia or in America.

Notes and coins used in China　　　　*Notes and coins used in Taiwan*

❀ Department stores and markets

Chinese people like fresh food, so most people buy what they need in the market every day. Apart from local markets, there are also shops and department stores. In Taiwan, all shops are privately run. In China, most department stores are operated by the goverment because of the communist system. Prices in these stores are fixed, and no bargaining is practised. However, many free markets are now privately run, and fruit, fish, meat, live chickens and groceries are sold, and bargaining is normally practised as in some markets in Taiwan.

A scene in a free market

dì liù kè bàifǎng péngyou
第六课 拜访朋友

1 Inviting

大伟，明天是星期六，你有空吗？

有啊！有什么事吗？

到我家玩儿，好吗？上午我们可以看录像带，下午游泳。

好啊！

你住哪儿？我写下来。

我住皇后街三十五号。

你家的电话号码是多少？

明天几点？

我家的号码是五六七八三九二。

上午十点半。

好。明天见。

2 Visiting

星期六…

你找哪位？

我找王小明。请问他在家吗？

他在。你请进。

谢谢。

你是小明的同学吗？

是。我叫白大伟。

来，请喝茶。

谢谢您。

你等一下。小明在浴室，他马上出来。

3 Introducing

嘿！大伟，你来了。

对不起，小明，我迟到了。

没关系。

来，我给你们介绍一下。
这是我的同学白大伟。

这是我爸爸、妈妈。

叔叔、阿姨好！

你好，大伟。欢迎你来。

4 Leaving

时间不早了。我该走了。
shíjiān　　　　gāi zǒu

妈！大伟要走了。

阿姨我走了。谢谢您的招待。
āyí　　　　　zhāodài

在这儿吃晚饭嘛！
ma

不用了。谢谢您。今天太打扰您了。
yòng　　　　dǎrǎo

不用客气，有空常来玩儿。
yòng kèqi　　　cháng

谢谢你，小明，今天游泳真过瘾。
yóuyǒng　guòyǐn

下星期日再来吧！
zài

太打扰了吧？
dǎrǎo

不会。我们都欢迎你来。可以吗？
dōu huānyíng

行。下星期日我再来。

Learn the sentences

❋ Asking if someone is available

To ask if someone is available, use either 有空吗 yǒu kòng ma or 有没有空 yǒu méi yǒu kòng. To answer yes, say 有 yǒu; to answer no, say 没有 méi yǒu. 没有 méi yǒu is often shortened as 没 méi in a statement, e.g. 我没空 Wǒ méi kòng.

你明天有空吗？	没有。
你今天下午有空吗？	有。
你后天有没有空？	我后天没空。
你星期天有空吗？	^{duìbuqǐ} 对不起，我没空。
你九月十三日有空吗？	^a 有啊！有什么事吗？

❋ Asking where someone lives

To ask Where do you live? say 你住在哪儿？ Nǐ zhù zài nǎr? The 在 zài is optional in oral conversation. To answer, replace the question word 哪儿 nǎr with the place name.

你住哪儿？	^{Mò'ěrběn} 我住墨尔本。
他住哪儿？	^{Niǔyuē} 他住纽约。
你爸爸住在哪儿？	^{Bùlǐsībān} 他住在布里斯班。
你妈妈住在哪儿？	^{Xīní} 她住在悉尼。

❋ Asking someone's telephone number

To ask someone's telephone number, use the question word 多少 duōshǎo. To answer the question, replace 多少 duōshǎo with the number.

你家的电话号码是多少？	我家的电话是三七八五六六五。
hàomǎ	
你家的电话是多少？	五六九六四六四。
他家的电话是多少？	他家电话是八九〇一二三四。
	yāo
她家的电话是多少？	好像是六四〇五五三三。
	hǎoxiàng

✳ Asking where someone works

To ask Where do you work? say 你在哪儿工作？Nǐ zài nǎr gōngzuò? To answer the question, replace 哪儿工作 nǎr gōngzuò with the place and type of work.

你在哪儿工作？	我在中学教书。
	jiāoshū
你爸爸在哪儿工作？	他在银行上班。
	yínháng shàngbān
他在哪儿工作？	他在白宫上班。
	Báigōng
你姐姐在哪儿工作？	她是护士，在医院上班。
	hùshi yīyuàn

✳ Asking if someone is home

To ask if someone is home, use either 在家吗 zài jiā ma or 在不在家 zài bú zài jiā. To reply yes to the question, say 在 zài; to reply no, say 不在 bú zài.

请问他在家吗？	他在。
请问他在不在家？	他不在。
你妈妈在家吗？	在。我去叫她。
你弟弟在不在家？	在。你等一下，我去叫他。
你明天在不在家？	在啊！有什么事吗？
	a

✳ **Use of** 一下 yíxià

一下 yíxià is sometimes used after a verb to indicate that action is short in duration. To say wait a minute or wait a while say 等一下 děng yíxià.

> 请你等一下，我马上回来。
>
> 来，我给你们介绍一下。
> jièshào
>
> 给我看一下，可以吗？

✳ **Polite expressions used when visiting**

Expressions a host uses when a visitor arrives:	
huānyíng 欢迎你来。	谢谢。
吃饭了吗？	吃了，谢谢。

Expressions a host uses when a visitor is leaving:	
cháng 有空常来玩儿。	好。
màn 慢走。	

Expressions a visitor uses when leaving:	
zhāodài 谢谢您的招待。	kèqi 不要客气。
dǎrǎo 太打扰您了。	yòng kèqi 哪里，不用客气。

【小笑话】
xiàohua

Wáng　　　　　ménkǒu　Lǐ　　tánhuà　tán
王太太在她家门口和李太太谈话，谈了两个小时。

王先生问他：“你为什么不请李太太进来坐？”

dá
王太太回答：“李太太说她没有时间。”

New words and expressions

拜访	bàifǎng	to visit
空	kòng	free time, spare time
玩儿	wánr	to play, to have fun　wán- to play; (é)r- [a word ending]
录像带	lùxiàngdài	video, video cassette　lù- to record; xiàng- image; dài- cassette
住	zhù	to live
写下来	xiě xiàlai	to write down　xiě- to write; xiàlai- to come down
皇后	huánghòu	queen
街	jiē	street
号码	hàomǎ	number　hào- number, date
找	zhǎo	to look for
哪位	nǎ/něi wèi	which one (person)　哪 is often pronounced as něi when directly followed by a measure word
来	lái	[to invite someone to do something]; to come
等	děng	to wait
一下	yíxià	a short while
马上	mǎshàng	right away　mǎ- horse; shàng- on, up
出来	chūlai	to come out　chū- to go or to come out; lái- to come
介绍	jièshào	to introduce
叔叔	shūshu	a form of address for a man of about one's father's age; father's younger brother
阿姨	āyí	a form of address for a woman of about one's mother's age; (in southern China) mother's sister
欢迎	huānyíng	welcome
黄金海岸	Huángjīn Hǎi'àn	Gold Coast　huángjīn- gold; hǎi'àn- coast
父亲	fùqin	father

工作	gōngzuò	work; to work
布里斯班	Bùlǐsībān	Brisbane
上班	shàngbān	to go to work　shàng- to go to, up; bān- duty, class
母亲	mǔqin	mother
中学	zhōngxué	high school (primary school – 小学 xiǎoxué, university – 大学 dàxué)
教书	jiāoshū	to teach (at school)　jiāo- to teach; shū- book
时间	shíjiān	(concept of) time　shí- hour; jiān- within
走	zǒu	to leave, to go
招待	zhāodài	to receive (guests); reception
不用	búyòng	need not　bù- not; yòng- to use
打扰	dǎrǎo	to disturb, to trouble
常	cháng	often
过瘾	guòyǐn	to one's heart's content, fully enjoyed
再	zài	again
会	huì	will; can, be able to
事	shì	thing, business; matter
墨尔本	Mò'ěrběn	Melbourne
纽约	Niǔyuē	New York
悉尼	Xīní	Sydney (said as 雪梨 xuělí in Taiwan)
银行	yínháng	bank　yín- silver; háng- business, firm
白宫	Báigōng	the White House　bái- white; gōng- palace
医院	yīyuàn	hospital
慢走	mànzǒu	to walk slowly and take care
笑话	xiàohua	joke　xiào- to laugh; huà- speech, talk
门口	ménkǒu	doorway　mén- door; kǒu- mouth
谈话	tánhuà	to have conversation, to talk, to chat
谈	tán	to talk, to chat
小时	xiǎoshí	hour (time duration)
问	wèn	to ask
为什么	wèishénme	why
进来	jìnlai	to come in　jìn- to enter; lái- to come
坐	zuò	to sit
回答	huídá	to answer　huí- to return; dá- to answer
说	shuō	to say

Write the characters

空 kòng *free time*	玩 wán *to play, to have fun*	住 zhù *to live*	电 diàn *electricity*	话 huà *speech*
请 qǐng *please; to invite*	问 wèn *to ask*	进 jìn *to enter*	等 děng *to wait*	出 chū *to come/go out*
时 shí *time, hour*	间 jiān *within; [measure word]*	该 gāi *should*	走 zǒu *to go, to leave, to walk*	再 zài *again*

everyoneloveswangli•everyoneloveswangli•everyoneloveswangli•everyoneloveswangli•everyoneloveswangli•everyoneloveswangli•everyoneloveswangli•everyoneloveswangli•everyoneloveswangli•everyoneloveswangli•everyoneloveswangli•everyoneloveswangli•everyoneloveswangli•everyoneloveswangli•everyoneloveswangli

马上回来

星期六上午十一点，林朋去找王

利，可是王利不在家。王利的妹妹在

家。她说王利和妈妈去百货商店买一双
　　　　　　 bǎihuò shāngdiàn　　 shuāng

皮鞋，马上回来。她请林朋进去客厅
píxié　　　　　　　　　　　　 kètīng

坐，也请他喝茶。林朋介绍他自己，说他是王利
zuò　　　　　 chá　　 jièshào　 zìjǐ

的同班同学，住在学校对面，他父亲和
 tóngbān　　　　 xuéxiào　　　　 fùqin

母亲都在学校教书。
mǔqin dōu　 xuéxiào jiāoshū

　　下午三点，林朋说他该走了。王利的

妹妹说："你再等一下，王利马上回来。"

Something to know

❀ Addressing friends' parents

It is considered rude to call older people by their names in Chinese society. There are polite forms of address, which vary from place to place. The most common forms used by children to address their friends' parents or parents' friends are shūshu 叔叔 and āyí 阿姨. Shūshu is a term used for the younger brothers of the father, but is used here to address males of one's parents' generation, while āyí is used for females. In some areas, bóbo 伯伯, a term for the father's older brother, and bómǔ 伯母, a term for his wife, are used if the person looks obviously much older than one's parents. In Taiwan and in some southern areas, the surname followed by māmā 妈妈 is often used for married females.

❀ Open your gift?

When visiting, it is common for the guest to present a gift to the host. This gift can be a cake, a basket of fruit, or a little toy for the children. However, it is a Chinese custom that the host does not unwrap the present in front of the visitor as this is regarded as impolite. The host is expected to welcome the visitor, but not to be looking forward to receiving presents. Although most overseas Chinese have adopted the Western custom of unwrapping presents as soon as they are received, those who have recently come from China or Taiwan still tend to maintain tradition.

❀ Would you like a cup of coffee?

During a formal visit, if the host asks the guest: Would you like a cup of coffee? Yào bú yào hē bēi kāfēi 要不要喝杯咖啡？the reply will normally be no, bú yào 不要, even if the guest is hot and thirsty. Chinese regard saying I would love to, wǒ yào 我要, as impolite. Saying no means that the guest does not want to cause the host too much trouble. Chinese drink tea at home rather than coffee. Normally, the host will offer the guest some tea, a cold drink, or fruit without asking.

1 A wrong number

2 Not home

三九七四二五八。  喂！
请问是三九七四二五八吗？

是。您找谁？

我找李兰兰。请问她在不在家？

兰兰不在家。您是哪位？

我是兰兰的同学。我叫白大伟。
请问，兰兰什么时候回来？

兰兰和美怡去游泳了，
下午三点左右回来。

那我下午再打来。您是李叔叔？

是的。

再见，李叔叔。

再见。

3 Wait a moment, please

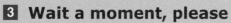

wèi
喂！

wèi
喂！李叔叔好！我是白大伟。

大伟，你好。你找兰兰？

是的。她回来了吗？

回来了。你等一会儿，我去叫她。

好的。谢谢您。

兰兰！你的电话。你的同学白大伟找你。

好，我马上来。

你等一会儿，兰兰马上来。

好的。谢谢您，李叔叔。

4 Speaking

喂 wèi
喂！是兰兰吗？

喂 wèi

是啊 a，我就 jiù 是。
有什么事吗，大伟？

你明天可以和我一起去中国城 chéng 吗？

你要去中国城做什么？

shuāng gōngfu　xié
我想去买一双功夫鞋。

你喜欢功夫鞋啊？

是啊！功夫鞋穿起来很舒服 shūfu。

好吧！可是我明天没空，后天可以吗？

后天也可以。

zhōng
几点钟？

中午十二点，可以吗？我来接 jiē 你。

wèntí
没问题。后天见。

 **Learn the sentences**

※ **Asking who is speaking on the telephone**

To ask Who is speaking? say 您是哪位？ Nín shì nǎ/něi wèi? To answer, say your name or your relationship to the person being sought.

您是哪位？	我是小王。 (Wáng)
您是哪位？	我是兰兰的同学。
您是哪位？	我是李叔叔。
请问您是哪位？	我是王阿姨。 (Wáng āyí)

※ **Asking someone who he/she is looking for**

To ask Who are you looking for? say 你找谁？ Nǐ zhǎo shéi? or more politely say 您找哪位？ Nín zhǎo nǎ/nei wèi? To answer, replace 谁 shéi or 哪位 nǎ/něi wèi with the person's name or title.

你找谁？	我找白先生。
您找哪位？	我找李太太。
您找哪位？	我找林老师。 (Lín)

喂！我找林老师，请问他在不在？

✻ Asking to talk to someone on the telephone

To ask to speak to a certain person on the telephone, ask whether the person is home. For example, in Lesson 6, we learnt to ask Is Lanlan home? say 兰兰在家吗？Lánlan zài jiā ma? or 兰兰在不在家？Lánlan zài bú zài jiā? Alternatively, we can say 我找兰兰 Wǒ zhǎo Lánlan, which means I'm looking for Lanlan.

我找大伟。	我就(jiù)是。
我找兰兰。请问她在不在？	她在。我去叫她。
我找美怡(Měiyí)。请问她在家吗？	她不在。您是哪位？
我找小明。请问他在家吗？	对不起，你打错号码(hàomǎ)了。

✻ Asking if someone has come back

To ask Has he come back? say 他回来了吗？Tā huílai le ma? To answer yes, say 他回来了。Tā huílai le. To answer no, say 他还没回来。Tā hái méi huílai. Notice the use of 了 le for a completed action as learnt in Lesson 2.

请问，林(Lín)老师回来了吗？	他回来了。
大伟回来了吗？	他还没回来。
你哥哥回来了吗？	回来了。
你妹妹回来了吗？	还没。

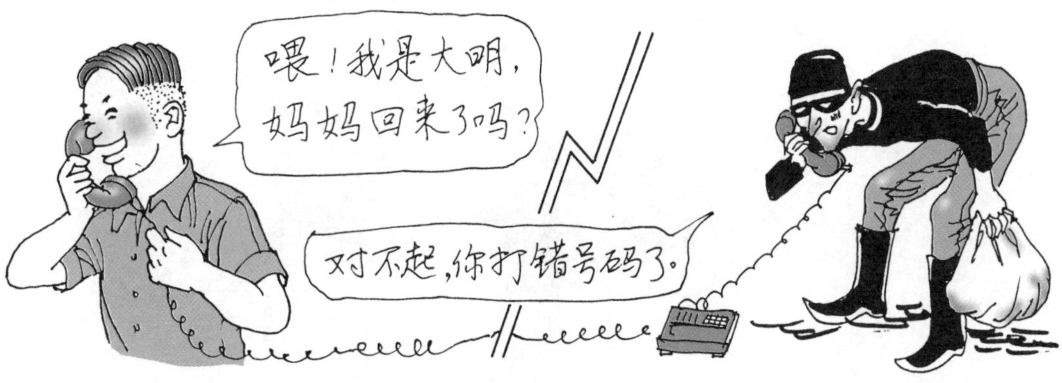

✳ **Asking when someone is coming back**

To ask When are you coming back? say 你什么时候回来？ Nǐ shénme shíhou huílai? when both the time and day are required. If only the time is needed, say 你几点回来？ Nǐ jǐ diǎn huílai?

他几点回来？	他十点左右回来。
你妈妈几点回来？	她下午两点半回来。
你什么时候回来？ <small>shíhou</small>	明天上午九点。
你爸爸什么时候回来？	他九月二十五号回来。

✳ **Asking someone the purpose of going somewhere**

To ask someone the purpose of going somewhere use 去 qù + verb + 什么 shénme.

你要去中国城做什么？	去买一双功夫鞋。
你要去纽约做什么？ <small>Niǔyuē</small>	去找朋友。
你去旧金山干什么？ <small>Jiùjīnshān　gàn</small>	去玩儿。
你要去书店买什么？ <small>shūdiàn</small>	去买一本字典。 <small>zìdiǎn</small>
你去百货商店买什么？ <small>bǎihuò shāngdiàn</small>	去买一条裤子。 <small>tiáo　kùzi</small>

说错话了

今天是老王的生日，他请了很多人去他家吃饭，时间是中午十二点。①

ài
唉！快十二点了！为什么该来的人还不来？

②

该来的人还不来！那么，我们是不该来的人啦！走了，我们走了。

③

yí
咦！为什么不该走的人走了？

④

不该走的人走了！那么，我们是该走的人啦！走，我们走了。

⑤

老王！你说错话了。大家都以为你不欢迎他们。
huānyíng

我说错话了？我不欢迎的不是他们。

⑥

你不欢迎的不是他们！那么，你不欢迎的是我啦！我走了！再见！

⑦

New words and expressions

喂	wèi	hello (on the telephone), hey
铃	líng	(telephone ringing sound); bell
左右	zuǒyòu	around, approximately zuǒ- left; yòu- right
一会儿	yíhuìr	a little while
我就是	wǒ jiù shì	I am (the person)
一起	yìqǐ	together
中国城	Zhōngguóchéng	Chinatown Zhōngguó- China; chéng- town
功夫鞋	gōngfu xié	Chinese soft shoes originally the footwear of the martial arts gōngfu- martial arts; xié- shoes
几点钟	jǐ diǎn zhōng	what time zhōng- clock
接	jiē	to meet, to pick (someone) up
没问题	méi wèntí	no problems
旧金山	Jiùjīnshān	San Francisco jiù- old; jīn- gold; shān- mountain
说话	shuōhuà	to speak
老王	Lǎo Wáng	Old Wang (Used to address an older friend whose surname is Wang) lǎo- old; wáng- king, a surname
啦	la	[exclamation]
入口	rùkǒu	entrance rù- to enter; kǒu- mouth
出口	chūkǒu	exit chū- to go out; kǒu- mouth
推	tuī	to push
拉	lā	to pull
男厕	náncè	men's toilet nán- male; cè- toilet
女厕	nǚcè	women's toilet nǚ- female

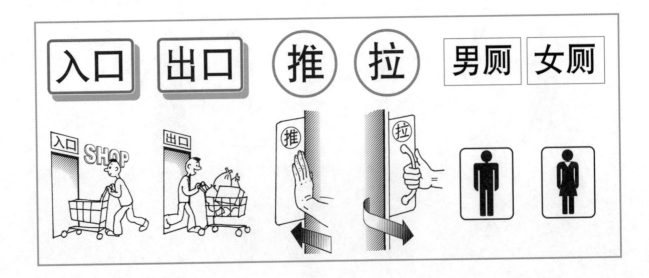

✎ Write the characters

伟 wěi *great*	兰 lán *orchid*	起 qǐ *to rise*	您 nín *you [polite form]*	李 lǐ *a surname; plum*
位 wèi *[measure word]*	叔 shū *one's father's younger brother*	候 hòu *time*	游 yóu *to swim*	泳 yǒng *swim*
城 chéng *town*	双 shuāng *pair*	功 gōng *skill*	夫 fū *man*	鞋 xié *shoes*

对 不 起

　　今天王利有空，他想找林朋到他家玩儿。上午十点半，他打电话给林朋，接(jiē)电话的是林朋的爸爸。他说林朋去中国城(chéng)买东西(dōngxi)，下午一点半左右回来。下午两点，王利再打电话，接(jiē)电话的是林朋的姐姐。她说林朋去买报纸(bàozhǐ)，马上回来。三点一刻(kè)，王利再打电话，接(jiē)电话的是林朋的妹妹。她说林朋在厕所(cèsuǒ)，请他等一下。三点四十分，林朋接(jiē)了电话，他说："对不起，王利，时间不早了，我不去你家了。"

Something to know

❀ Chinatown and Chinese migrants

The huge number and the wide dispersion of Chinese migrants is reflected in the saying "Where the sea reaches, there Chinese can be found". Chinese language is commonly used and the old customs are practised by overseas Chinese. This can be seen particularly in the Chinatowns in the big cities of many countries such as the United States, Canada, Japan and Australia. In Chinatown, Zhōngguóchéng 中国城, or sometimes called Tángrénjiē 唐人街, namely Chinese street, there are Chinese grocery stores, medicine shops, restaurants, gift shops etc.

Chinese migration dates back to 540 A.D., with around 7,000 families residing in Japan at that time. Most migrants left China after the 16th century, when Chinese labourers were transported by some Western countries to their colonies as coolies. Many people on the southeast coast of China, where the land is poor, moved to southeast Asia to seek a better living and gradually settled there. During the gold rush in the United States and in Australia, Chinese gold diggers went and sought their fortunes. Many of them settled in the United States. In Australia, the number of Chinese immigrants decreased dramatically after the introduction of the White Australia Policy, but still a small number settled down. Many Chinese started businesses such as laundries and restaurants and some are now working in every professional field in many countries. As most of these migrants are from southeastern China most of them speak the Cantonese dialect, Guǎngdōnghuà 广东话, but are able to read and write Chinese characters.

The recent wave of Chinese migrants in the 20th century are people from many different social backgrounds. They are postgraduate students who study and then are employed overseas, or more recently, businessmen who are operating successful businesses, and skilled persons who specialise in a particular professional area. Most of them are from Taiwan and Hong Kong, and some are students from China. As most of these recent migrants speak Mandarin, Mandarin is becoming more and more popular in the local community and in Chinatown. However, except for the small number of people from mainland China who migrated after the reform of the Chinese language, most overseas Chinese read and write traditional characters. Local Chinese newspapers and publications are mostly printed in the traditional form. While there are a few weekend schools using simplified characters, most are still using the traditional form.

dì bā kè chīfàn
第八课 吃饭

1 A note to a friend

兰兰：

　　今天上午我来找你，^{gānghǎo}刚好你出去了。你妈妈说你去书店(shūdiàn)买书。下星期二是我的生日。我爸爸、妈妈要带(dài)我去中国饭馆(fànguǎn)吃饭。我想请你也一起去，时间是下午六点半，不知道(zhīdao)你有没有空？请你回家后打电话给我。

大伟 留(liú)

二〇〇二年七月十三日上午十点

2 We often go to a restaurant

大伟，对不起，因为我昨天很晚回家，所以没给你打电话。

没关系。你星期二可以去吗？

可以，谢谢你的邀请。

你们常上中国馆子吗？

常啊。我们一家人常常上馆子。我尤其喜欢去饮茶。

YUM CHA

我也喜欢饮茶，可是我们不常上馆子。
我妈妈菜做得很好。

你在家都吃中国菜吗？

平常都吃中国菜，
有时候也吃牛排。

改天请你到我们家吃便饭。

3 Eating at a restaurant

今天大伟、爸爸和妈妈请兰兰到中国饭馆吃饭。

请坐，您想吃点儿什么？

今天我点菜。请给我菜单。(càidān)
来一盘古老肉(pán gǔlǎoròu)，一盘麻婆豆腐(mápó dòufu)，
一碗狮子头(wǎn shīzitóu)，还有两份春卷(fèn chūnjuǎn)。

要喝什么汤(tāng)？

给我们一大碗酸辣汤(wǎn suānlàtāng)。

4 Eating at home

今天兰兰请大伟到她家吃饭。

吃饭了。

chéng
我来盛饭。

大伟，来，随便坐。
suíbiàn zuò

谢谢。

大伟，没什么菜，
你自己来。别客气。
zìjǐ　　bié kèqi

不客气，我自己来。
zìjǐ
阿姨菜做得真好。
āyí

你太客气了，大伟。

真的，这柠檬鸡片真好吃。
níngméng jīpiàn

那多吃点儿。再添一碗饭吧？
tiān　　wǎn

不了。我吃得太饱了。
bǎo

 **Learn the sentences**

※ **Explaining cause**

To state a cause and its consequence, use 因为 yīnwèi......所以 suǒyǐ...... or just use 所以 suǒyǐ...... alone.

> 因为我昨天很晚回家，所以没给你打电话。
>
> 因为他今天很晚起床，所以迟到了。
> <small>qǐchuáng　　　　　chídào</small>
>
> 我快迟到了，所以没吃早饭。
> <small>kuài chídào</small>
>
> 今天的菜很好吃，所以我吃得很饱。
> <small>bǎo</small>
>
> 这葡萄太酸了，所以他不吃。
> <small>pútao　　suān</small>

※ **Expressing *usually* or *often***

To say that someone usually does something, use 平常 píngcháng. For example, to say I usually get up early, say 我平常都很早起床。Wǒ píngcháng dōu hěn zǎo qǐchuáng. To say that someone does something often, use 常常 chángchang or 常 cháng and to say not often, use 不常 bù cháng. For example, to say I often go swimming, say 我常去游泳。Wǒ cháng qù yóuyǒng; to say I don't go swimming often, say 我不常去游泳。Wǒ bù cháng qù yóuyǒng.

平常 usually	我们平常都吃中国菜。
	我平常都很早起床。
常常；常 often	我们常常上馆子。
	我星期天常去游泳。
不常 not often	我不常上馆子。
	我不常去百货商店。 <small>bǎihuò shāngdiàn</small>

✳ **Offering a choice**

When offering a choice, use 还是 háishi which means or. To ask Do you want to eat boiled rice or fried rice? say 你要吃米饭还是炒饭？ Nǐ yào chī mǐfàn háishi chǎofàn?

您要吃米饭还是炒饭？	炒饭。
chènshān　　　hànshān 你要买衬衫还是汗衫？	chènshān 我要买衬衫。
你要红色的还是白色的？	我要白色的。
lánqiú 你要去打篮球还是去游泳？	lánqiú 去打篮球。
gōngkè 他在看小人儿书还是在做功课？	看小人儿书。
你喜欢游泳还是打球？	我喜欢打球。
tiáo qúnzi　féi　　shòu 这条裙子太肥还是太瘦？	shòu 太瘦了。

New words and expressions

刚好	gānghǎo	just, happen to
出去	chūqu	to go out chū- to go out; qù- to go
带……去	dài...qù	to take... to dài- to take, to bring; qù- to go
饭馆	fànguǎn	restaurant, or said 餐馆 cānguǎn
后	hòu	after; back, behind
留	liú	to leave (a note)
因为	yīnwèi	because yīn- cause; wèi- for
回家	huíjiā	to go home huí- to return; jiā- home
所以	suǒyǐ	therefore suǒ- so; yǐ- to use
邀请	yāoqǐng	to invite
常常	chángchang	often
馆子	guǎnzi	restaurant, used more often in southern China, going to a restaurant – 上馆子 shàng guǎnzi
尤其	yóuqí	especially

饮茶	yǐnchá	yumcha, a Cantonese meal of small snacks and tea
		yǐn- to drink; chá- tea
平常	píngcháng	usually píng- smooth; cháng- often, usually
有时候	yǒushíhou	sometimes
牛排	niúpái	steak niú- cow, bull; pái(gǔ)- spareribs
改天	gǎitiān	some other day gǎi- to change; tiān- day
便饭	biànfàn	[modest form] a simple meal biàn- convenient
点菜	diǎncài	to order food diǎn- to choose, hour; cài- dish, vegetable
菜单	càidān	menu cài- dish, vegetable; dān- list
来……	lái...	give (us/me) ... (used when ordering food)
盘	pán	[a measure word for dish] plate
麻婆豆腐	mápó-dòufu	name of a hot and spicy bean curd dish, said to be named
		after a woman who was skilled in cooking this dish
		mápó- old woman with a pockmarked face; dòufu- bean curd
碗	wǎn	[a measure word for rice or soup] bowl
狮子头	shīzitóu	name of a dish of fried meatballs shīzi- lion; tóu- head
汤	tāng	soup
酸辣汤	suānlàtāng	hot and sour soup suān- sour; là- hot
米饭	mǐfàn	plain rice, called 白饭 báifàn in Taiwan
		mǐ- uncooked rice
还是	háishi	or
炒饭	chǎofàn	fried rice chǎo- to stir-fry
对了	duìle	by the way
放	fàng	to put; to let off, to let go
味精	wèijīng	monosodium glutamate (M.S.G.)
客人	kèrén	guest kè- guest; rén- person
多	duō	more, a lot
结帐	jiézhàng	to settle an account
盛饭	chéngfàn	to serve rice, to fill a bowl with rice
随便坐	suíbiàn zuò	sit anywhere suíbiàn- to do as one pleases; zuò- to sit
自己来	zìjǐ lái	to help oneself zìjǐ- self; lái- to help, do, come
别客气	bié kèqi	don't stand on ceremony; don't be formal;
		make yourself at home kèqi- courteous
不客气	bú kèqi	not being courteous; not at all; you are welcome
添	tiān	to add
饱	bǎo	to be full

Write the characters

因	为	所	常	馆
yīn *cause, reason*	wèi *for*	suǒ *so; place*	cháng *often*	guǎn *shop, building*
子	饮	茶	都	平
zi *[suffix]*	yǐn *to drink*	chá *tea*	dōu *all*	píng *smooth*
客	气	米	炒	得
kè *guest*	qì *manner; air*	mǐ *uncooked rice*	chǎo *to stir-fry*	de *[degree, result of]*

everyoneloveswangli•everyoneloveswangli•everyoneloveswangli•everyoneloveswangli•everyoneloveswangli•everyoneloveswangli•everyoneloveswangli

做 得 很 好

　　林朋喜欢吃炒饭，可是学校不卖炒饭。他
在学校平常都吃三明治、汉堡包和热狗。上星
期四中午吃饭时，林朋说他很想吃炒饭。王利
说他会做炒饭，他可以早上在家里
做，中午请林朋吃。

　　　　　　　　星期五早上，因为王利很晚
起床，所以他去学校旁边的中国
馆子买了炒饭，中午请林朋吃。现
在林朋常常说："王利炒饭做得很
好。"

在此小便

A man urinated at a street corner where the sign 行人等不得在此小便 could be clearly seen. This sign is read as "行人等，不得在此小便。Xíngrén děng, bù dé zài cǐ xiǎobiàn." It means *Pedestrians etc. cannot urinate here*.

He was caught by a policeman. The policeman asked him: "Didn't you see the sign there?" The man answered: "Yes. That's why I did it. You see, it says 行人，等不得，在此小便。Xíngrén, děng bù dé, zài cǐ xiǎobiàn." The way this man read the sign change the meaning into *Pedestrians who cannot wait urinate here*.

From this sign we can see that some words have different meanings from what we have learnt. On the sign, 行人 xíngrén means *pedestrians*; 等 děng means *et cetera*; 不得 bù dé means *cannot*; 此 cǐ means *here*; and 小便 xiǎobiàn means *urine or to urinate*. When the man read the sign he used 等 děng meaning *wait* instead of meaning *et cetera*.

Now we have learnt that 小便 xiǎobiàn means *urine or to urinate*. Can you work out what 大便 dàbiàn means?

Something to know

✿ Food balance

Chinese believe that food contains the nature of yīn 阴 or yáng 阳, that is, having *the properties of cooling or warming*. Cooling foods such as bean curd, watermelon, celery and green tea often contain less calories while warming foods such as cherries, ginger, chilli, meat and black tea often contain more calories. Cooking methods can alter the cooling or warming nature of food. For example, deep-fried foods tend to be warming and pickled foods are cooling. A balance of cooling and warming foods is important in the Chinese diet.

✿ Bean curd in Chinese diet

Bean curd, dòufu 豆腐, which is made from soybeans and is high in protein, is a favourite of most Chinese. Not having much flavour in itself, dòufu combines well with almost any ingredients to produce a great variety of tastes. It can be steamed, boiled, deep-fried, or shallow-fried. Dòfu is used in simple cooking for the family daily meal while it can also be a luxurious dish for a special occasion. The popular hot and spicy dish mápó dòufu 麻婆豆腐 is said to have been invented by a pockmarked-faced widow who ran a little restaurant for a living. The term mápó means *pockmarked-faced old woman*.

❀ Family meal

The family meal is generally simpler than that at a restaurant. The staple food is rice in southern China and wheat products in northern China. Although meals vary from place to place and from day to day, a typical breakfast may consist of rice porridge with eggs and pickled vegetables, or soybean milk with sesame seed cakes, shāobǐng 烧饼, and deep-fried dough sticks, yóutiáo 油条. For lunch, it could be a bowl of noodle soup and for dinner, rice or steamed buns with vegetables, soup and meat or fish.

The Chinese habitually have their rice and other dishes first and the soup last. However, most Chinese restaurants overseas have adopted the Western style and serve the soup at the beginning of the meal.

When guests are invited for a meal at home, the Chinese often use modest words at the table. Wǒ tàitai bú huì zuò cài 我太太不会做菜, Cài zuò de bù hǎo 菜做得不好, or Méi shénme cài 没什么菜, are commonly used although there may be a full table of their best cooking.

❀ Formal feast

A formal Chinese feast commonly consists of 10 to 12 courses, starting with a cold dish and ending with a sweet dish. The seating arrangement is regarded as important at a formal feast, although it is not normally practised for a daily meal at home. At a round table, the seat facing the door is for the guest of honour and the seat with the back to the door is the host's. Couples normally sit together. This arrangement and the short distance over the round table facilitates conversation between the guest and the host.

Seat of host

Seats of hosts

Formal table seating

dì　jiǔ　kè　　tiānqì
第 九 课 天 气

1 **What's the weather today?** 今天天气怎么样？

xiàyǔ
今天下雨。

xiàxuě
今天下雪。

guā　fēng
今天刮大风。

今天天气很好。

rè
今天很热。

lěng
今天很冷。

liángkuài
今天很凉快。

2 Beijing's weather

一年有四季。每季有三个月。

北京的春天是三月到五月；夏天是六月到八月；

秋天是九月到十一月；冬天是十二月到二月。

北京的春天很暖和，但是常常刮风；

冬天很冷，但是不常下雪。

北京的夏天很热，是游泳的好季节；

秋天很凉爽，是游览的好季节。

3 Weather report

昨天的天气：
阴，午后有雨。
_{zuìgāo} _{qìwēn} _{shèshì} _{dù}
最高气温摄氏二十九度，
_{zuìdī} _{dù}
最低二十四度。

_{yùbào}
今天的天气预报：
_{qíng} _{léizhènyǔ}
上午晴，下午有雷阵雨。
_{qìwēn} _{shèshì} _{dù}
最高气温摄氏三十二度，

最低二十五度。

_{yùbào}
明天的天气预报：
_{yún}
晴，有时多云。
_{qìwēn} _{shèshì}
最高气温摄氏三十四度，

最低二十八度。

4 It's raining again

昨天晚上又(yòu)下雨了。

真的啊(a)！我一点儿都不知道(zhīdao)。
我大概(dàgài)睡(shuì)得太死(sǐ)了。现在还下雨吗？

现在雨停(tíng)了。

今天我想去游泳。你去不去？

不去。我还想睡觉(shuìjiào)。

天气预报(yùbào)说今天会很热。

多热？最高气温(qìwēn)多少？

三十六度。起床(qǐchuáng)！去游泳吧！

好吧！

(After breakfast) 真讨厌(tǎoyàn)！又(yòu)下雨了。

太好了。下雨天是睡觉天，我再去睡觉(shuìjiào)。

Learn the sentences

※ **Inquiring about the weather**

To ask What's the weather like today? say 今天天气怎么样？ Jīntiān tiānqì zěnmeyàng? To answer, state the condition, such as It's raining today. say 今天下雨。Jīntiān xiàyǔ; and It is cold today. say 今天很冷。Jīntiān hěn lěng.

今天天气怎么样？	今天下雨。
	今天很冷。
昨天天气怎么样？	昨天刮大风。
	昨天天气很好，很凉快 *liángkuài*
明天天气怎么样？	明天会下雪。
	明天会很热。

※ **Use of 会 huì to indicate the future**

The word 会 huì is often used to describe something which is going to or likely to happen in the future. For example, to say It's going to rain tomorrow, say 明天会下雨。Míngtiān huì xiàyǔ.

明天天气怎么样？	明天会下雨。
	天气预报说明天会很冷。 *yùbào*
你看明天会下雨吗？	大概不会吧！ *dàgài*
兰兰下午会回来吗？	会，她下午三点回来。
林老师明天会走吗？	他明天不会走。

110

✳ Use of 到 dào **to indicate length of time**

The word 到 dào is used to indicate a duration of time and is equivalent to the English word to. To say January to February, say 一月到二月 yī yuè dào èr yuè .

北京的春天：	三月到五月
澳大利亚的春天：	九月到十一月
上学的时间：	上午九点到下午三点
看电视的时间： diànshì	晚上七点到七点半
做功课的时间： gōngkè	晚上七点半到九点半

✳ Use of 死 sǐ **to describe an extreme condition**

The word 死 sǐ, which literally means to die or dead, can also be used in conversation as a stative verb to describe an extreme condition. Therefore, to express I'm starving (extremely hungry), say 我饿死了。Wǒ è sǐ le.

> 我睡得太死了。
> shuì　　sǐ
>
> 我饿死了！我们去吃点儿东西吧！
> sǐ　　　　　　dōngxi
>
> 今天热死了。
> sǐ

【小笑话】
xiàohua

老林在小王家做客。因为下雨，老林住了很多天还
Lín　　　Wáng
不走，所以小王写了一首诗："下雨天留客天留我不留"
shǒu shī　　　liú
他的意思是："下雨天留客，天留，我不留。"老林看
yìsi　　　　　　　　　　　　　　　　　　　　Lín
到这首诗，他念："下雨天，留客天，留我不？留。"
shǒu shī　　　niàn
他很高兴，又多住了几天。
gāoxìng

New words and expressions

天气	tiānqì	weather tiān- sky, day; qì- air
下雨	xiàyǔ	to rain xià- (of rain or snow) to fall, under; yǔ- rain
下雪	xiàxuě	to snow xià- (of rain or snow) to fall, under; xuě- snow
刮风	guāfēng	windy (extremely windy – 刮大风 guā dà fēng) guā- to blow; fēng- wind
热	rè	hot
冷	lěng	cold
凉快	liángkuài	cool and pleasant liáng- cool; kuài- happy, fast
季	jì	season
每	měi	every
北京	Běijīng	the capital city of China běi- north; jīng- capital
春天	chūntiān	spring chūn- spring; tiān- sky, day
到	dào	to, until; to reach
夏天	xiàtiān	summer xià- summer; tiān- sky, day
秋天	qiūtiān	autumn qiū- autumn; tiān- sky, day
冬天	dōngtiān	winter dōng- winter; tiān- sky, day
暖和	nuǎnhuo	warm
但是	dànshì	but, however
季节	jìjié	season jì- season; jié- section, festival
凉爽	liángshuǎng	cool and pleasant liáng- cool; shuǎng- pleasant
游览	yóulǎn	to go sight-seeing
阴	yīn	cloudy (cloudy day – 阴天 yīntiān)
午后	wǔhòu	afternoon wǔ- noon; hòu- after
最高	zuìgāo	highest zuì- the most; gāo- high
气温	qìwēn	temperature qì- air; wēn- temperature, warm
摄氏	shèshì	centigrade (Fahrenheit – 华氏 huáshì)
度	dù	degree
最低	zuìdī	lowest zuì- the most; dī- low
预报	yùbào	forecast yù- in advance; bào- report
晴	qíng	fine; fine day – 晴天 qíngtiān
雷阵雨	léizhènyǔ	thunder shower léi- thunder; zhènyǔ- shower

有时	yǒushí	sometimes
多云	duōyún	cloudy　duō- a lot, more; yún- cloud
又	yòu	again
死	sǐ	deathly; dead; to die
停	tíng	to stop
多热	duō rè	How hot?
讨厌	tǎoyàn	annoying; to hate　tǎo- to incur; yàn- to be disgusted with
老李	Lǎo Lǐ	Old Li
小王	Xiǎo Wáng	Little Wang
做客	zuòkè	to be a guest　zuò- to be, to do; kè- guest
首	shǒu	[a measure word for poem]
诗	shī	poem
意思	yìsi	meaning
念	niàn	to read
高兴	gāoxìng	happy　gāo- high; xìng- excitement
几天	jǐtiān	a few days　jǐ- an uncertain number, how many; tiān- day

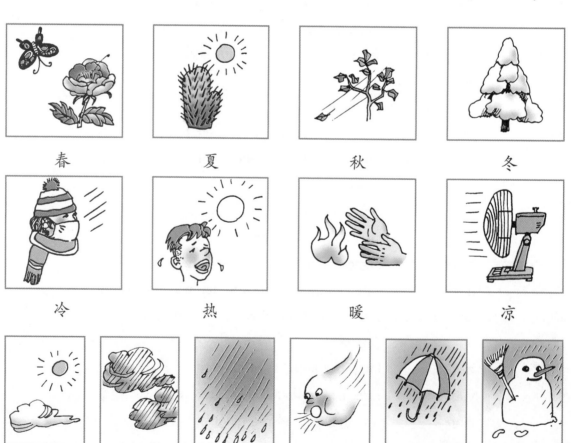

春　　　　　夏　　　　　秋　　　　　冬

冷　　　　　热　　　　　暖　　　　　凉

晴天　　　阴天　　　雨天　　　刮风　　　下雨　　　下雪

Write the characters

雨 yǔ *rain*	雪 xuě *snow*	刮 guā *to blow (wind)*	风 fēng *wind*	热 rè *hot*
冷 lěng *cold*	凉 liáng *cool*	春 chūn *spring*	夏 xià *summer*	秋 qiū *autumn, fall*
冬 dōng *winter*	北 běi *north*	京 jīng *capital*	暖 nuǎn *warm*	阴 yīn *cloudy*
晴 qíng *sunny*	最 zuì *the most*	高 gāo *high*	低 dī *low*	度 dù *degree*

everyoneloveswangli•everyoneloveswangli•everyoneloveswangli•everyoneloveswangli

别去了
bié

早上林朋到王利家，他们要一起去打
网球。今天天气很热，林朋到的时候气温是
wǎngqiú　　　　　　　　　　　　　　　qìwēn
摄氏三十八度。王利说："这么热，别去打网
shèshì　　　　　　　　　　　　　　bié
球了。我看，我们上午在家看电视，下午去游
　　　　　　　　　　　diànshì
泳。"吃午饭的时候，电视的天气预报说，下
　　　　　　　　diànshì　　yùbào
午有雷阵雨，会刮大风和下大雨。王利说："我
léizhènyǔ　　guā
看，别去游泳了。我们看录像带吧！"
bié　　　　　　lùxiàngdài

Something to know

❀ Climate in China

Due to the vastness of the country, the weather in China varies dramatically from region to region. The country covers a total area of approximately 9.6 million square kilometres with mountains in the west and plains in the east. The climate ranges from frigid in the north to tropical in the south. The average annual rainfall is 1,500 mm in the humid southeast and only 50 mm in the arid northwest. The hottest area in summer is in Turpan, Tǔlǔfān 吐鲁番, in Xīnjiāng 新疆 where the average daytime temperature in July exceeds 40°C. The coldest area is in the Hǎilār 海拉尔 district in Inner Mongolia, Nèi Měnggǔ 内蒙古, where the average temperature in January is -27.7°C. Hēilóngjiāng 黑龙江 province is entirely without summer, and Hǎinán Island 海南岛 is virtually without winter. In the Huáihé 淮河 basin, the four seasons are clearly defined, while in Kūnmíng 昆明, it is springlike all year round.

❀ Key tourist spots in China

With a vast land and a long history, China has plentiful physical and cultural attractions. Tourists are fascinated by the beautiful scenery of the ancient sacred mountains: Tàishān 泰山 in Shāndōng 山东 province and Huàshān 华山 in Shǎnxī 陕西 province. Visitors to Tàishān can climb up 7,000 steps to its peak to admire the beauty of nature. West Lake, Xīhú 西湖, in Hángzhōu 杭州 was a favourite topic for ancient poets and still displays poetic beauty. The limestone pinnacles in Guìlín 桂林 and the Stone Forest, Shílín 石林, in Yúnnán 云南 province, exhibit the fantastic craft of nature.

The Buddhist murals and statues in the caves of Dūnhuáng 敦煌 and Yúngāng 云冈, and the giant 71-metre high Buddha at the hill of Lèshān 乐山 are masterpieces of human endeavour. The unearthed terracotta warriors in Xī'ān 西安 are representative of the empire of Qín Shǐhuáng 秦始皇.

A scene of the limestone pinnacles along the Li River in Guìlín 桂林

The giant Buddha in Lèshān 乐山

Chángchéng 长城, the Great Wall

In Běijīng 北京, the renovated section of the Great Wall, Chángchéng 长城, in Bādálǐng 八达岭 tells of the history of Chinese expansion. The Forbidden City, Zǐjìnchéng 紫禁城, presents the magnificence of the ancient palace, and Fragrance Hill, Xiāngshān 香山, displays its splendid red foliage in fall.

❀ Key tourist spots in Taiwan

An island smaller than Tasmania with its highest mountain at 3950 metres provides Taiwan with spectacular scenery. Taroko Gorge, Tàilǔgé 太鲁阁, at the entrance of the Cross-island Highway, Héngguàn Gōnglù 横贯公路, features a magnificent marble gorge; Ali mountain, Ālǐshān 阿里山, displays a turbulent sea of clouds and a beautiful sunrise; The National Chungshan Museum, Zhōngshān Bówùyuàn 中山博物院 (or briefly called Gùgōng 故宫) shows the abundant treasures of Chinese culture.

Zhōngshān Bówùyuàn 中山博物院 in Taipei, Taiwan

dì shí kè fùxí rìjì
第十课 复习（日记）

1 A diary

二〇〇二年十二月七日，星期六，晴

今天是星期六，天气很好。上午很凉快(kuài)，可是

下午非常(fēicháng)热。

我今天很早起床(qǐchuáng)。上午我和妈妈去百货商店(bǎihuò shāngdiàn)买

东西。妈妈的皮鞋(píxié)坏(huài)了，她买了一双(shuāng)黑色的皮鞋(píxié)。

我的裤子(kùzi)破(pò)了，我买了一条(tiáo)白色的裤子(kùzi)。中午我们

到中国馆子饮茶。我们一家人常常上馆子吃中国菜，

我尤其(yóuqí)喜欢去饮茶。

今天是美怡(Měiyí)的生日。下午三点，兰兰和我请她

看电影(diànyǐng)。美怡(Měiyí)今天穿一条(tiáo)浅(qiǎn)黄色的连衣裙(liányīqún)，看起来

很漂亮(piàoliang)；兰兰穿红衬衫(chènshān)、黑裙子(qúnzi)，非常(fēicháng)时髦(shímáo)。

明天早上六点我和爸爸去钓鱼(diàoyú)。今天晚上要

早点儿睡觉(shuìjiào)。

2 Language Functions

[1]　Asking the date

今天是几月几号？ Jīntiān shì jǐ yuè jǐ hào?

今天是三月八号。 Jīntiān shì sān yuè bā hào.

Asking the day of the week

今天是星期几？ Jīntiān shì xīngqī jǐ?

今天是星期三。 Jīntiān shì xīngqīsān.

Asking the year someone was born

你是哪年生的？ Nǐ shì nǎ nián shēng de?

我是一九六九年生的。 Wǒ shì yī jiǔ liù jiǔ nián shēng de.

Asking for permission

我明天去看电影，可以吗？ Wǒ míngtiān qù kàn diànyǐng, kěyǐ ma?

可以。 Kěyǐ.　or　不行。 Bù xíng.

Asking about birthdays

你的生日是什么时候？ Nǐ de shēngrì shì shénme shíhou?

我的生日是七月十四号。 Wǒ de shēngrì shì qī yuè shísì hào.

Stating the date

今天是一九九三年十二月一日，星期三。

Jīntiān shì yī jiǔ jiǔ sān nián shí'èr yuè yī rì, xīngqīsān.

[2]　Finding out what someone is doing

你在做什么？ Nǐ zài zuò shénme?

我在做功课。 Wǒ zài zuò gōngkè.

Asking the time

现在几点？ Xiànzài jǐ diǎn?

现在七点十五分。 Xiànzài qī diǎn shíwǔ fēn.

Asking what time someone does something

你几点上学？ Nǐ jǐ diǎn shàngxué?

我八点半上学。 Wǒ bā diǎn bàn shàngxué.

Use of "了 le"

好了！好了！ Hǎo le! Hǎo le!

太好了。 Tài hǎo le.

我的书包坏了。 Wǒ de shūbāo huài le.

你迟到了。 Nǐ chídào le.

他来了。 Tā lái le.

[3]　Asking the location of something

请问，厕所在哪儿？ Qǐngwèn, cèsuǒ zài nǎr?

在最后面。 Zài zuì hòumian.

Asking what someone is doing somewhere

他在客厅做什么？ Tā zài kètīng zuò shénme?

看电视。 Kàn diànshì.

Asking where someone is doing something

他在哪里做功课？ Tā zài nǎli zuò gōngkè?

在电视机前面！ Zài diànshìjī qiánmian!

Asking what happened

怎么回事？ Zěnme huí shì?

他的裤子破了。 Tā de kùzi pò le.

Finding out where someone sleeps

你昨天晚上睡哪儿？ Nǐ zuótiān wǎnshang shuì nǎr?

睡客厅沙发。 Shuì kètīng shāfā.

[4] Asking what someone is wearing

她今天穿什么衣服？ Tā jīntiān chuān shénme yīfu?

她穿黄色的连衣裙。 Tā chuān huángsè de liányīqún.

Describing how clothes fit

这双皮鞋太小了。 Zhè shuāng píxié tài xiǎo le.

这件旗袍很合身。 Zhè jiàn qípáo hěn héshēn.

Use of "起来 qǐlai" after the verb

这双功夫鞋穿起来很舒服。 Zhè shuāng gōngfu xié chuān qǐlai hěn shūfu.

这条裙子看起来很漂亮。 Zhè tiáo qúnzi kàn qǐlai hěn piàoliang.

Wondering what to wear

我明天该穿什么衣服呢？ Wǒ míngtiān gāi chuān shénme yīfu ne?

你该穿西装。 Nǐ gāi chuān xīzhuāng.

Asking for an opinion

你看这件衬衫怎么样？ Nǐ kàn zhè jiàn chènshān zěnmeyàng?

挺好看的。 Tǐng hǎokàn de.

Use of "有没有 yǒu méi yǒu" for a past event

你今天有没有吃早饭？ Nǐ jīntiān yǒu méi yǒu chī zǎofàn?

有，我吃了。 Yǒu, wǒ chī le.　or　我没吃。 Wǒ méi chī.

[5] Asking the price

这本书多少钱？ Zhè běn shū duōshǎo qián?　三块半。 Sān kuài bàn.

苹果怎么卖？ Píngguǒ zěnme mài?　一斤一块四。 Yì jīn yí kuài sì.

Asking if something is for sale

你们卖字典吗？ Nǐmen mài zìdiǎn ma?

卖。 Mài.　or　不卖。 Bú mài.

你们有没有字典？ Nǐmen yǒu méi yǒu zìdiǎn?

有。 Yǒu.　or　没有。 Méi yǒu.

Expressing an opinion on goods or asking for a choice

这个挺好的，可是太贵了。 Zhè gè tǐng hǎo de, kěshì tài guì le.

这件衬衫太大了，有没有小点儿的？

Zhè jiàn chènshān tài dà le, yǒu méi yǒu xiǎo diǎnr de?

Asking whether something is sweet or sour

葡萄甜不甜（酸不酸）？ Pútao tián bù tián (suān bù suān)?

很甜。 Hěn tián.　or　不酸。 Bù suān.

[6] Asking if someone is available

你明天有空吗？ Nǐ míngtiān yǒu kòng ma?

有。 Yǒu.　or　没有。 Méi yǒu.

Asking where someone lives

你住哪儿？ Nǐ zhù nǎr? 我住悉尼。 Wǒ zhù Xīní.

Asking someone's telephone number

你家的电话号码是多少？ Nǐ jiā de diànhuà hàomǎ shì duōshǎo?

九八七六五四三。 Jiǔ bā qī liù wǔ sì sān.

Asking if someone is home

请问他在家吗？ Qǐngwèn tā zài jiā ma?

在。 Zài. or 不在。 Bú zài.

Use of "一下 yíxià"

请你等一下，他马上来。 Qǐng nǐ děng yíxià, tā mǎshàng lái.

来，我给你们介绍一下。 Lái, wǒ gěi nǐmen jièshào yíxià.

[7] **Asking who is speaking on the phone**

您是哪位？ Nín shì nǎ /něi wèi?

我是大伟的同学。 Wǒ shì Dàwěi de tóngxué.

Asking someone who he/she is looking for

你找谁？ Nǐ zhǎo shéi?

我找李老师。 Wǒ zhǎo Lǐ lǎoshī.

Asking to talk to someone on the phone

我找林老师，请问他在家吗？ Wǒ zhǎo Lín lǎoshī, qǐngwèn tā zài jiā ma?

我就是。 Wǒ jiù shì. or 在。 Zài. or 不在。 Bú zài.

Asking if someone has come back

请问兰兰回来了吗？ Qǐngwèn Lánlan huílai le ma?

回来了。 Huílai le. or 还没回来。 Hái méi huílai.

Asking when someone is coming back

他几点回来？ Tā jǐ diǎn huílai?

下午四点半。 Xiàwǔ sì diǎn bàn.

Asking someone the purpose of going somewhere

你去他家做什么？ Nǐ qù tā jiā zuò shénme? 去玩儿。 Qù wánr.

[8] **Explaining cause**

因为我太晚起床，所以没吃早饭。

Yīnwèi wǒ tài wǎn qǐchuáng, suǒyǐ méi chī zǎofàn.

Offering a choice

你要去游泳还是打球？ Nǐ yào qù yóuyǒng háishi dǎqiú?

我要去游泳。 Wǒ yào qù yóuyǒng. or 我要去打球。 Wǒ yào qù dǎqiú.

[9] **Inquiring about the weather**

今天天气怎么样？ Jīntiān tiānqì zěnmeyàng?

今天很热。 Jīntiān hěn rè.

明天会下雨吗？ Míngtiān huì xiàyǔ ma?

会。 Huì. or 不会。 Bú huì.

Stating the length of time

北京的春天：三月到五月。 Běijīng de chūntiān: sān yuè dào wǔ yuè.

吃午饭的时间：下午十二点半到一点半。

Chī wǔfàn de shíjiān: xiàwǔ shí'èr diǎn bàn dào yì diǎn bàn.

Use "死 sǐ" to describe an extreme condition

我饿死了。 Wǒ è sǐ le.

今天热死了。 Jīntiān rè sǐ le.

Appendix 1

WORDS AND EXPRESSIONS
Chinese-English

m.w.- measure word

Simplified	Pinyin	English	Traditional	Lesson
A 阿姨	āyí	[*address*] woman of one's mother's age; (in Taiwan) mother's sister	阿姨	6
唉	ài	(a sigh)	唉	6
B 白	bái	white	白	4
白饭	báifàn	(in Taiwan) plain rice	白飯	8
白宫	Báigōng	White House	白宮	6
白色	báisè	white	白色	4
百货商店	bǎihuò shāngdiàn	department store	百貨商店	5
拜访	bàifǎng	to visit	拜訪	6
半	bàn	half	半	2
半夜	bànyè	midnight	半夜	3
饱	bǎo	to be full	飽	8
报纸	bàozhǐ	newspaper	報紙	5
北京	Běijīng	the capital city of China	北京	9
本	běn	[*m.w.* - book, magazine etc.]	本	5
便饭	biànfàn	[modest form] a simple meal	便飯	8
表	biǎo	watch	錶	2
别客气	bié kèqi	don't be formal; make yourself at home	別客氣	8
冰箱	bīngxiāng	refrigerator	冰箱	4
菠萝	bōluó	pineapple, also called 凤梨 fènglí	菠蘿	5
不客气	bú kèqi	not being courteous; not at all; you are welcome	不客氣	8
不用	búyòng	need not	不用	6
布里斯班	Bùlǐsībān	Brisbane	布里斯班	6
C 猜	cāi	to guess	猜	3
菜单	càidān	menu	菜單	8
草莓	cǎoméi	strawberry	草莓	5
厕所	cèsuǒ	toilet, lavatory	廁所	3
差	chà	differ from	差	2
长	cháng	long	長	4
常	cháng	often	常	6
常常	chángchang	often	常常	8
唱歌	chànggē	to sing	唱歌	3
炒饭	chǎofàn	fried rice	炒飯	8
车	chē	car, vehicle	車	3
车库	chēkù	garage	車庫	3

120

Simplified	Pinyin	English	Traditional	Lesson
车子	chēzi	car, small vehicle	車子	4
衬衫	chènshān	shirt	襯衫	4
盛饭	chéng fàn	to serve rice, to fill a bowl with rice	盛飯	8
橙色	chéngsè	orange (colour)	橙色	4
迟到	chídào	to arrive late	遲到	2
出来	chūlai	to come out	出來	6
出口	chūkǒu	exit	出口	7
出去	chūqu	to go out	出去	8
厨房	chúfáng	kitchen	廚房	3
穿	chuān	to wear (clothes, shoes or socks)	穿	4
穿起来	chuān qǐlai	impression or feeling of the clothes on someone	穿起來	4
串	chuàn	[m.w. - bananas, grapes] bunch, cluster	串	5
春天	chūntiān	spring	春天	9
从	cóng	to follow; from	從	3
错	cuò	wrong, incorrect	錯	1
D 打	dǎ	to play (ball game, taichi etc.);	打	3
		to dial (telephone)		3
打扰	dǎrǎo	to disturb, to trouble	打擾	6
大便	dàbiàn	excrement; to empty the bowels	大便	8
大概	dàgài	probably	大概	1
大人	dàrén	adults	大人	3
大学	dàxué	university	大學	6
袋	dài	bag	袋	5
带……去	dài...qù	to take ... to	帶……去	8
蛋糕	dàngāo	cake	蛋糕	1
但是	dànshì	but; however	但是	9
倒霉	dǎoméi	to have bad luck	倒霉	3
到	dào	to go to, to arrive;	到	5
		to, until		9
等	děng	to wait	等	6
地板	dìbǎn	floor	地板	3
地图	dìtú	map	地圖	5
点	diǎn	o'clock; dot;	點	2
		to choose (food)		8
点菜	diǎncài	to order food	點菜	8
点儿	diǎnr	a little	點兒	5
电冰箱	diànbīngxiāng	refrigerator	電冰箱	3
电话	diànhuà	telephone	電話	3
电视	diànshì	television	電視	3
电视机	diànshìjī	television set	電視機	3
电影	diànyǐng	movie	電影	2
钓鱼	diàoyú	to fish	釣魚	1
顶	dǐng	[m.w. - hat, cap]	頂	5
冬天	dōngtiān	winter	冬天	9
都	dōu	already; all	都	3

Simplified	Pinyin	English	Traditional	Lesson
度	dù	degree (temperature)	度	9
短	duǎn	short (length)	短	4
短裤	duǎnkù	shorts	短褲	4
对	duì	right, correct	對	1
对了	duìle	by the way	對了	8
对面	duìmian	opposite (location)	對面	3
多	duō	more, a lot; how	多	8
多热	duō rè	how hot	多熱	9
多少	duōshǎo	how much, how many	多少	5
多云	duōyún	cloudy	多雲	9

F 饭馆	fànguǎn	restaurant	飯館	8
饭厅	fàntīng	dining room	飯廳	3
房子	fángzi	house	房子	3
放	fàng	to let off, to let go, to release;	放	2
		to put		8
放学	fàngxué	to finish classes (classes are over)	放學	2
非常	fēicháng	extremely	非常	5
肥	féi	loose-fitting (clothing); fat	肥	4
分	fēn	minute;	分	2
		one-cent unit = 0.01 块 kuài or 元 yuán		5
份	fèn	[m.w. - newspaper, copy etc.]	份	5
风	fēng	wind, breeze	風	9
风筝	fēngzhēng	kite	風箏	2
凤梨	fènglí	pineapple	鳳梨	5
父亲	fùqin	father	父親	6

G 该	gāi	should	該	2
改天	gǎitiān	some other day	改天	8
干	gàn	to do, to work	幹	2
刚好	gānghǎo	just, happen to	剛好	8
高兴	gāoxìng	happy	高興	9
给	gěi	to give	給	5
功夫鞋	gōngfu xié	Chinese soft shoes	功夫鞋	7
功课	gōngkè	school work, homework	功課	2
公寓	gōngyù	flat, unit	公寓	3
工作	gōngzuò	work; to work	工作	6
咕噜肉	gūlūròu	sweet and sour pork	咕嚕肉	8
古老肉	gǔlǎoròu	sweet and sour pork	咕咾肉	8
刮风	guāfēng	windy	刮風	9
馆子	guǎnzi	restaurant	館子	8
贵	guì	expensive, dear	貴	5
过瘾	guòyǐn	to one's heart's content, fully enjoyed	過癮	6

| **H** 还 | hái | also; still | 還 | 3 |
| 还不错 | hái búcuò | [oral] not bad, pretty good | 還不錯 | 5 |

Simplified	Pinyin	English	Traditional	Lesson
还是	háishi	or	還是	8
汗衫	hànshān	undershirt, T-shirt	汗衫	4
汉英字典	Hàn-Yīng zìdiǎn	Chinese-English dictionary	漢英字典	5
好了好了	hǎo le hǎo le	that's enough	好了好了	1
好看	hǎokàn	good-looking	好看	4
好像	hǎoxiàng	seem, be like	好像	4
号	hào	date; number	號	1
号码	hàomǎ	number	號碼	8
喝茶	hē chá	to have tea	喝茶	2
合身	héshēn	well-fitting (clothing)	合身	4
黑色	hēisè	black	黑色	4
红	hóng	red	紅	4
后	hòu	after; back, behind	後	8
后面	hòumian	behind	後面	3
后年	hòunián	the year after next	後年	1
后天	hòutiān	the day after tomorrow	後天	1
花园	huāyuán	garden	花園	3
华氏	Huáshì	Fahrenheit	華氏	9
坏	huài	broken down; bad	壞	3
欢迎	huānyíng	welcome	歡迎	6
皇后	huánghòu	queen	皇后	6
黄金海岸	Huángjīn Hǎi'àn	Gold Coast	黃金海岸	6
黄色	huángsè	yellow	黃色	4
回答	huídá	to answer	回答	6
回家	huíjiā	to go home	回家	8
回来	huílai	to come back, to return	回來	3
会	huì	will; can, be able to	會	6

J

Simplified	Pinyin	English	Traditional	Lesson
几点钟	jǐ diǎn zhōng	what time	幾點鐘	7
几天	jǐtiān	a few days	幾天	9
季	jì	season	季	9
季节	jìjié	season	季節	9
间	jiān	[m.w. - room]; within (time, space)	間	3, 6
见	jiàn	to see, to catch sight of	見	3
件	jiàn	[m.w. - clothing or affair]	件	4
教书	jiāoshū	to teach (at school)	教書	6
角	jiǎo	[formal] 10-cent unit	角	5
街	jiē	street	街	6
接	jiē	to meet, to pick (someone) up	接	7
结帐	jiézhàng	to settle an account	結帳	8
介绍	jièshào	to introduce	介紹	6
斤	jīn	a unit of weight = 0.5 kilograms	斤	5
今年	jīnnián	this year	今年	1
今天	jīntiān	today	今天	1
进来	jìnlai	to come in	進來	6
进去	jìnqu	to go in, to enter	進去	2

Simplified	Pinyin	English	Traditional	Lesson
旧	jiù	old (nonliving thing), worn	舊	3
旧金山	Jiùjīnshān	San Francisco	舊金山	7
橘子	júzi	mandarin, tangerine	橘子	5
K 咖啡色	kāfēisè	brown	咖啡色	4
看	kàn	to look at, to see, to watch; to think	看	2, 4
看到	kàndào	to catch sight of, to see	看到	4
看看	kànkan	to have a look	看看	4
看起来	kàn qǐlai	looks, impression or feeling of the look	看起來	4
可是	kěshì	but, however	可是	5
可以	kěyǐ	can, may	可以	1
刻	kè	a quarter (of an hour)	刻	2
客人	kèrén	guest	客人	8
客厅	kètīng	living room, lounge	客廳	3
空	kòng	free time, spare time	空	6
裤子	kùzi	trousers, pants	褲子	4
块	kuài	[oral] monetary unit for dollar	塊	5
快	kuài	nearly; fast, hurry	快	2
快乐	kuàilè	happy	快樂	1
宽	kuān	loose-fitting (clothing) (used in Taiwan)	寬	4
L 拉	lā	to pull	拉	7
啦	la	[exclamation]	啦	7
来	lái	[to invite someone to do something]; to come	來	1
来……	lái...	give me/us... (when ordering food)	來……	8
蓝	lán	blue	藍	4
老李	Lǎo Lǐ	Old Li	老李	9
老王	Lǎo Wáng	Old Wang	老王	7
了	le	[grammatical word]	了	1
雷阵雨	léizhènyǔ	thunder shower	雷陣雨	9
冷	lěng	cold	冷	9
里面	lǐmian	inside	裡面	3
荔枝	lìzhī	lychee	荔枝	5
连衣裙	liányīqún	woman's dress	連衣裙	4
凉快	liángkuài	cool and pleasant	涼快	9
凉爽	liángshuǎng	cool and pleasant	涼爽	9
零	líng	zero	零	5
铃	líng	(telephone ringing sound); bell	鈴	7
另外	lìngwài	in addition, besides	另外	3
留	liú	to leave (a note);	留	8
		to keep		9
楼房	lóufáng	multi-storey building	樓房	3
录像带	lùxiàngdài	video, video cassette	錄像帶	6
绿色	lùsè	green	綠色	4
M 麻婆豆腐	mápó-dòufu	name of a hot and spicy bean curd dish	麻婆豆腐	8

Simplified	Pinyin	English	Traditional	Lesson
马上	mǎshàng	right away	馬上	6
嘛	ma	[word ending - indicates an obvious situation]	嘛	4
买	mǎi	to buy	買	1
卖	mài	to sell	賣	5
慢	màn	slow	慢	2
慢走	màn zǒu	to walk slowly and take care	慢走	6
毛	máo	[oral] 10-cent unit = 0.1 块 kuài	毛	5
毛衣	máoyī	sweater	毛衣	4
帽子	màozi	hat, cap	帽子	5
没问题	méi wèntí	no problems	沒問題	7
每	měi	every	每	9
门口	ménkǒu	doorway	門口	6
谜语	míyǔ	riddle	謎語	3
米饭	mǐfàn	plain rice	米飯	8
棉袄	mián'ǎo	cotton-padded coat	棉襖	4
明年	míngnián	next year	明年	1
明天	míngtiān	tomorrow	明天	1
墨尔本	Mò'ěrběn	Melbourne	墨爾本	6
母亲	mǔqin	mother	母親	6
N 哪	nǎ	which, what	哪	1
哪儿	nǎr	[oral] where	哪兒	3
哪位	nǎ/něi wèi	which one (person)	哪位	6
那	nà	[conj.] then; that	那	5
那么	nàme	then	那麼	1
男厕	náncè	men's toilet	男廁	7
念	niàn	to read	唸	9
您	nín	[polite form] you	您	6
牛排	niúpái	steak	牛排	8
纽约	Niǔyuē	New York	紐約	6
暖和	nuǎnhuo	warm	暖和	9
女厕	nǚcè	women's toilet	女廁	7
O 喔	ō	[to express surprise/understanding] oh	喔	1
哦	ò	[to indicate realization] oh	哦	1
P 盘	pán	[m.w. - dish]; plate	盤	8
旁边	pángbian	the side	旁邊	4
配	pèi	to match	配	4
朋友	péngyou	friend	朋友	6
皮鞋	píxié	leather shoes	皮鞋	4
篇	piān	[m.w. - short writing]	篇	10
便宜	piányi	cheap, inexpensive	便宜	5
漂亮	piàoliang	pretty	漂亮	4
平常	píngcháng	usually	平常	8
平房	píngfáng	single-storey house	平房	3

Simplified	Pinyin	English	Traditional	Lesson
苹果	píngguǒ	apple	蘋果	5
破	pò	broken, torn	破	3
葡萄	pútao	grapes	葡萄	5
Q 旗袍	qípáo	close-fitting dress with a high neck and slit skirt	旗袍	4
起床	qǐchuáng	to get up, to get out of bed	起床	2
气温	qìwēn	temperature	氣溫	9
钱	qián	money	錢	5
前面	qiánmian	front	前面	3
前年	qiánnián	the year before last	前年	1
前天	qiántiān	the day before yesterday	前天	1
浅	qiǎn	light (colour); shallow	淺	4
晴天	qíngtiān	fine day, sunny day	晴天	9
请	qǐng	to invite; please	請	1
请进	qǐngjìn	come in please	請進	6
秋天	qiūtiān	autumn	秋天	9
去	qù	to go	去	1
去年	qùnián	last year	去年	1
裙子	qúnzi	skirt	裙子	4
R 热	rè	hot	熱	9
日	rì	day; the sun	日	1
日常	rìcháng	day-to-day, daily	日常	2
日记	rìjì	diary	日記	10
入口	rùkǒu	entrance	入口	7
S 沙发	shāfā	sofa (transliteration of sofa)	沙發	3
上	shàng	on top of, up; to go to; first part	上	3
上班	shàngbān	to go to work	上班	6
上(个)星期	shàng (gè) xīngqī	last week	上(個)星期	1
上个月	shàng gè yuè	last month	上個月	1
上面	shàngmian	above, on top of	上面	3
上午	shàngwǔ	morning	上午	2
上学	shàngxué	to go to school	上學	1
摄氏	shèshì	centigrade	攝氏	9
深	shēn	dark (colour); deep	深	4
生	shēng	to be born, to give birth to; pupil	生	1
生活	shēnghuó	life	生活	2
生日	shēngrì	birthday	生日	1
诗	shī	poem	詩	9
狮子头	shīzitóu	a dish of fried meatballs	獅子頭	8
时候	shíhou	time, moment	時候	1
时间	shíjiān	(concept of) time	時間	6
时髦	shímáo	fashion, fashionable	時髦	4
市场	shìchǎng	market	市場	5
首	shǒu	[m.w. - poem]	首	9

Simplified	Pinyin	English	Traditional	Lesson
瘦	shòu	tight-fitting (clothing); thin	瘦	4
书店	shūdiàn	bookshop	書店	5
书房	shūfáng	study	書房	3
舒服	shūfu	comfortable	舒服	4
叔叔	shūshu	[*address*] man of one's father's age; father's younger brother	叔叔	6
双	shuāng	[*m.w.* - shoes, socks etc.] pair	雙	4
双胞胎	shuāngbāotāi	twins	雙胞胎	1
水床	shuǐchuáng	water bed	水床	3
水果	shuǐguǒ	fruit	水果	5
睡	shuì	to sleep	睡	3
睡觉	shuìjiào	to sleep	睡覺	2
说	shuō	to say	說	6
说话	shuōhuà	to speak	說話	7
死	sǐ	deathly; dead, to die	死	9
送	sòng	to deliver, to send	送	3
送来	sòng lái	to deliver here	送來	3
送去	sòng qù	to send to	送去	3
酸	suān	sour	酸	5
酸辣汤	suānlàtāng	hot and sour soup	酸辣湯	8
随便坐	suíbiàn zuò	sit anywhere	隨便坐	8
所以	suǒyǐ	therefore	所以	8
T 太	tài	too (exceedingly)	太	3
太极拳	tàijíquán	taichi	太極拳	3
太太	tàitai	Mrs.; (in Taiwan) wife	太太	4
谈	tán	to talk, to chat	談	6
谈话	tánhuà	to have a conversation, to talk, to chat	談話	6
汤	tāng	soup	湯	8
讨厌	tǎoyàn	annoying; to hate	討厭	9
套	tào	[*m.w.* - clothing or furniture] set, suit	套	3
添	tiān	to add	添	8
天哪！	tiān na!	Good heavens!	天哪！	3
天气	tiānqì	weather	天氣	9
甜	tián	sweet	甜	5
条	tiáo	[*m.w.* - trousers, shorts, skirt, river etc.]	條	4
跳舞	tiàowǔ	to dance	跳舞	2
听	tīng	to listen, to hear	聽	2
停	tíng	to stop	停	9
挺	tǐng	[oral] very	挺	4
同	tóng	same, together	同	1
同学	tóngxué	classmate, schoolmate	同學	6
推	tuī	to push	推	7
W 袜子	wàzi	socks	襪子	4
外面	wàimian	outside	外面	3

Simplified	Pinyin	English	Traditional	Lesson
外套	wàitào	coat	外套	4
玩儿	wánr	to play, to have fun	玩兒	6
碗	wǎn	[m.w. - rice, noodle soup etc.] bowl	碗	8
晚	wǎn	late, evening	晚	3
晚饭	wǎnfàn	dinner	晚飯	2
晚上	wǎnshang	evening, night	晚上	2
王	Wáng; wáng	a surname; king	王	4
喂	wèi	hello (on the telephone), hey	喂	7
味精	wèijīng	monosodium glutamate (M.S.G.)	味精	8
为什么	wèishénme	why	為什麼	6
问	wèn	to ask	問	6
我就是	wǒ jiùshì	I am (the person); speaking (on the phone)	我就是	7
卧室	wòshì	bedroom	臥室	3
午饭	wǔfàn	lunch	午飯	2
午后	wǔhòu	afternoon	午後	9

	Simplified	Pinyin	English	Traditional	Lesson
X	悉尼	Xīní	Sydney	悉尼	6
	西装	xīzhuāng	Western-style attire, suit	西裝	4
	洗衣房	xǐyīfáng	laundry	洗衣房	3
	洗衣机	xǐyījī	washing machine	洗衣機	3
	下(个)星期	xià (gè) xīngqī	next week	下(個)星期	1
	下个月	xià gè yuè	next month	下個月	1
	下面	xiàmian	under, below	下面	3
	下棋	xiàqí	to play chess	下棋	2
	下午	xiàwǔ	afternoon	下午	2
	下星期日	xià xīngqīrì	next Sunday	下星期日	6
	下雪	xiàxuě	to snow	下雪	9
	下雨	xiàyǔ	to rain	下雨	9
	夏天	xiàtiān	summer	夏天	9
	先生	xiānsheng	Mr.; (in Taiwan) husband	先生	4
	现在	xiànzài	now, at present	現在	2
	香蕉	xiāngjiāo	banana	香蕉	5
	想	xiǎng	to feel like; to think	想	5
	小便	xiǎobiàn	to urinate; urine	小便	8
	小弟弟	xiǎo dìdi	little boy	小弟弟	4
	小姐	xiǎojiě	Miss; young lady	小姐	4
	小妹妹	xiǎomèimei	little girl	小妹妹	4
	小人儿书	xiǎorénrshū	[oral] children's picture-story book	小人兒書	2
	小时	xiǎoshí	hour (time duration)	小時	6
	小王	Xiǎo Wáng	Little Wang	小王	9
	小学	xiǎoxué	primary school	小學	6
	笑话	xiàohua	a joke	笑話	6
	鞋	xié	shoes	鞋	3
	写	xiě	to write	寫	2
	写下来	xiě xiàlai	to write down	寫下來	6
	新	xīn	new	新	3

Simplified	Pinyin	English	Traditional	Lesson
星期	xīngqī	week	星期	1
星期二	xīngqī'èr	Tuesday	星期二	1
星期六	xīngqīliù	Saturday	星期六	1
星期日	xīngqīrì	Sunday	星期日	1
星期三	xīngqīsān	Wednesday	星期三	1
星期四	xīngqīsì	Thursday	星期四	1
星期天	xīngqītiān	Sunday	星期天	1
星期五	xīngqīwǔ	Friday	星期五	1
星期一	xīngqīyī	Monday	星期一	1
行	xíng	all right, O.K.	行	1
修理	xiūlǐ	to repair, to fix	修理	3
雪梨	xuělí	Sydney	雪梨	6

Y 阳台	yángtái	balcony, veranda	陽台	3
邀请	yāoqǐng	to invite	邀請	8
要	yào	to be going to;	要	2
		to want		5
也	yě	also	也	1
衣服	yīfu	clothes, clothing	衣服	4
医生	yīshēng	doctor	醫生	6
医院	yīyuàn	hospital	醫院	6
一共	yígòng	all together	一共	5
一会儿	yíhuìr	a little while	一會兒	7
一下	yíxià	a short while	一下	6
一点儿都不	yìdiǎnr dōu bù	not at all...	一點兒都不	5
一起	yìqǐ	together	一起	7
已经	yǐjīng	already	已經	2
以为	yǐwéi	thought (mistakenly)	以為	1
意思	yìsi	meaning	意思	9
阴天	yīntiān	cloudy day	陰天	9
因为	yīnwèi	because	因為	8
音乐	yīnyuè	music	音樂	2
银行	yínháng	bank	銀行	6
饮茶	yǐnchá	yumcha - a Cantonese meal of small snacks and tea	飲茶	8
游览	yóulǎn	to go sightseeing	遊覽	9
游泳池	yóuyǒng chí	swimming pool	游泳池	3
尤其	yóuqí	especially	尤其	8
有时	yǒushí	sometimes	有時	9
有时候	yǒushíhou	sometimes	有時候	8
又	yòu	again	又	9
右边	yòubian	right (location)	右邊	3
预报	yùbào	forecast	預報	9
浴室	yùshì	bathroom, shower room	浴室	3
元	yuán	[formal] monetary unit for dollar	元	5
月	yuè	month; the moon	月	1

Simplified	Pinyin	English	Traditional	Lesson
Z 杂志	zázhì	magazine	雜誌	5
在	zài	[indicates an action in progress];	在	2
		at, in, on		3
再	zài	again	再	6
糟糕	zāogāo	[oral] oh no, how terrible	糟糕	2
早	zǎo	early, morning	早	3
早饭	zǎofàn	breakfast	早飯	2
早上	zǎoshang	(early) morning	早上	2
怎么	zěnme	how	怎麼	4
怎么回事	zěnme huí shì	what happened, what's the matter	怎麼回事	3
怎么样	zěnmeyàng	how about, what about	怎麼樣	4
窄	zhǎi	tight-fitting (clothing) (used in Taiwan), narrow	窄	4
招待	zhāodài	to receive, reception	招待	6
找	zhǎo	to look for;	找	4
		to give change		5
找到了	zhǎodào le	found	找到了	4
找找	zhǎozhao	to have a look for	找找	4
只	zhī	[m.w. - shoe, sock, animal]	隻	4
只有	zhǐyǒu	only	只有	7
中国城	Zhōngguóchéng	Chinatown	中國城	7
中午	zhōngwǔ	midday, noon	中午	2
中学	zhōngxué	high school	中學	6
祝	zhù	to wish	祝	1
住	zhù	to live	住	6
紫	zǐ	purple	紫	4
字	zì	character, word	字	2
字典	zìdiǎn	dictionary	字典	5
自己	zìjǐ	self	自己	4
自己来	zìjǐ lái	to help oneself	自己來	8
走	zǒu	to leave, to go	走	6
最	zuì	the most	最	3
最低	zuìdī	lowest	最低	9
最高	zuìgāo	highest	最高	9
昨天	zuótiān	yesterday	昨天	1
左边	zuǒbian	left (location)	左邊	3
左右	zuǒyòu	around	左右	7
坐	zuò	to sit	坐	6
做	zuò	to do, to make;	做	2
		to cook		8
做客	zuòkè	to be a guest	做客	9

Appendix 2

WORDS AND EXPRESSIONS
English-Chinese

English	Simplified	Pinyin
A		
a few days	几天	jǐtiān
a little	(一)点儿	(yì)diǎnr
a little while	一会儿	yíhuìr
a number of, some	一些	yìxiē
a quarter (of an hour)	一刻	yí kè
a short while	一下	yíxià
above, on top of	上面	shàngmian
action in progress	在	zài
afternoon	下午, 午后	xiàwǔ, wǔhòu
again	又, 再	yòu, zài
all	都	dōu
all right, O.K.	行	xíng
all together	一共	yígòng
already	已经	yǐjīng
also	也	yě
annoying; to hate	讨厌	tǎoyàn
answer	回答	huídá
apple	苹果	píngguǒ
around	左右	zuǒyòu
arrive late	迟到	chídào
ask	问	wèn
at, in, on	在	zài
autumn	秋天	qiūtiān
B		
bad; broken down	坏	huài
bag	袋	dài
balcony, veranda	阳台	yángtái
banana	香蕉	xiāngjiāo
bank	银行	yínháng
bathroom, shower room	浴室	yùshì
be a guest	做客	zuòkè
be born; give birth to	生	shēng
because	因为	yīnwèi
bedroom	卧室	wòshì
behind	后面	hòumian
Beijing	北京	Běijīng
birthday	生日	shēngrì

English	Simplified	Pinyin
black	黑(色)	hēi(sè)
blue	蓝(色)	lán(sè)
bookshop	书店	shūdiàn
breakfast	早饭	zǎofàn
Brisbane	布里斯班	Bùlǐsībān
broken down; bad	坏	huài
broken, torn	破	pò
brown	咖啡色	kāfēisè
but, however	但是, 可是	dànshì, kěshì
C		
can, may	可以	kěyǐ
car, vehicle	车	chē
centigrade	摄氏	shèshì
character, word	字	zì
chat, to talk	谈	tán
children's picture book	小人儿书	xiǎorénrshū
Chinatown	中国城	Zhōngguóchéng
Chinese-English dictionary	汉英字典	Hàn-Yīng zìdiǎn
Chinese soft shoes	功夫鞋	gōngfu xié
clothes, clothing	衣服	yīfu
cloudy	多云	duōyún
cloudy day	阴天	yīntiān
coat	外套	wàitào
cold	冷	lěng
come	来	lái
come back	回来	huílai
come in please	请进	qǐngjìn
come out	出来	chūlai
comfortable	舒服	shūfu
(completed action)	了	le
cook; do, make	做	zuò
cool and pleasant	凉快, 凉爽	liángkuài, liángshuǎng
correct	对	duì
cotton-padded coat	棉袄	mián'ǎo
D		
dance	跳舞	tiàowǔ

English	Simplified	Pinyin
dark (colour); deep	深	shēn
date; number	号	hào
day; the sun	日	rì
day after tomorrow	后天	hòutiān
day before yesterday	前天	qiántiān
dear, expensive	贵	guì
deathly; dead, die	死	sǐ
deep; dark (colour)	深	shēn
deliver, send	送	sòng
deliver here	送来	sòng lái
department store	百货商店	bǎihuò shāngdiàn
dictionary	字典	zìdiǎn
die	死	sǐ
differ from	差	chà
dining room	饭厅	fàntīng
dinner	晚饭	wǎnfàn
disturb, to trouble	打扰	dǎrǎo
do	做	zuò
doctor	医生	yīshēng
don't be formal, make yourself at home	别客气	bié kèqi
doorway	门口	ménkǒu
dot	点	diǎn
dress - close fitting with a high neck and slit skirt	旗袍	qípáo

E

English	Simplified	Pinyin
early	早	zǎo
eat	吃	chī
entrance	入口	rùkǒu
especially	尤其	yóuqí
evening, night	晚上	wǎnshang
everyone	大家	dàjiā
(exclam. - realization)	哦	ò
(exclam. - surprise; understanding)	喔	ō
excrement	大便	dàbiàn
exit	出口	chūkǒu
expensive, dear	贵	guì
extremely	非常	fēicháng

F

English	Simplified	Pinyin
Fahrenheit	华氏	huáshì
fashion, fashionable	时髦	shímáo
fast; hurry	快	kuài
fat	肥	féi

English	Simplified	Pinyin
father	父亲	fùqin
father's younger brother	叔叔	shūshu
feel like; think	想	xiǎng
feel with the wearing	穿起来	chuān qǐlai
fine day, sunny day	晴天	qíngtiān
finish classes	放学	fàngxué
fish (v.)	钓鱼	diàoyú
fix, repair	修理	xiūlǐ
flats, units	公寓	gōngyù
floor	地板	dìbǎn
follow	从	cóng
forecast	预报	yùbào
found	找到了	zhǎodào le
free time, spare time	空	kòng
Friday	星期五	xīngqīwǔ
fried rice	炒饭	chǎofàn
friend	朋友	péngyou
front	前面	qiánmian
fruit	水果	shuǐguǒ

G

English	Simplified	Pinyin
garage	车库	chēkù
garden	花园	huāyuán
get up, get out of bed	起床	qǐchuáng
give	给	gěi
give birth to; be born	生	shēng
give change	找	zhǎo
give us... (ordering food)	来……	lái...
go	去	qù
go home	回家	huíjiā
go in, enter	进去	jìnqu
go out	出去	chūqu
go sightseeing	游览	yóulǎn
go to	上	shàng
go to school	上学	shàngxué
go to work	上班	shàngbān
go to, arrive	到	dào
going to	要	yào
Gold Coast	黄金海岸	Huángjīn Hǎi'àn
Good heavens!	天哪！	tiān na!
good-looking	好看	hǎokàn
grapes	葡萄	pútao
green	绿(色)	lù(sè)
guess	猜	cāi
guest	客人	kèrén

English	Simplified	Pinyin
H		
half	半	bàn
happy	高兴,	gāoxìng,
	快乐	kuàilè
hat, cap	帽子	màozi
hate; annoying	讨厌	tǎoyàn
have a conversation, chat	谈话	tánhuà
have a look	看看	kànkan
have a look for	找找	zhǎozhao
have a meal	吃饭	chīfàn
have bad luck	倒霉	dǎoméi
have tea	喝茶	hē chá
hello (on the phone), hey	喂	wèi
help oneself	自己来	zìjǐ lái
highest	最高	zuìgāo
homework	功课	gōngkè
hospital	医院	yīyuàn
hot	热	rè
hot and sour soup	酸辣汤	suānlàtāng
hour (time duration)	小时	xiǎoshí
house	房子	fángzi
how	怎么	zěnme
how about, what about	怎么样	zěnmeyàng
how hot	多热	duō rè
how much, how many	多少	duōshǎo
however, but	但是, 可是	dànshì, kěshì
husband (in Taiwan); Mr.	先生	xiānsheng
I		
I am (the person); speaking	我就是	wǒ jiù shì
in addition, besides	另外	lìngwài
in, at, on	在	zài
incorrect	错	cuò
inside	里面	lǐmian
introduce	介绍	jièshào
invite	邀请	yāoqǐng
invite; please	请	qǐng
J		
just, happen to	刚好	gānghǎo
K		
keep	留	liú
king; a surname	王	wáng; Wáng
kitchen	厨房	chúfáng
kite	风筝	fēngzhēng

English	Simplified	Pinyin
L		
last month	上个月	shàng gè yuè
last week	上(个)星期	shàng (gè) xīngqī
last year	去年	qùnián
late, evening	晚	wǎn
laundry	洗衣房	xǐyīfáng
leather shoes	皮鞋	píxié
leave (a note)	留	liú
leave, go	走	zǒu
left (location)	左边	zuǒbian
let off, let go, release	放	fàng
life	生活	shēnghuó
light (colour); shallow	浅	qiǎn
listen, hear	听	tīng
little boy	小弟弟	xiǎo dìdi
little girl	小妹妹	xiǎo mèimei
Little Wang	小王	Xiǎo Wáng
live	住	zhù
living room	客厅	kètīng
long	长	cháng
look at, see, watch	看	kàn
look for	找	zhǎo
looks	看起来	kàn qǐlai
loose-fitting (clothing)	肥, 宽	féi, kuān
lowest	最低	zuìdī
lunch	午饭	wǔfàn
lychee	荔枝	lìzhī
M		
m.w. - book, magazine	本	běn
m.w. - clothing, affair	件	jiàn
m.w. - clothing, furniture (set)	套	tào
m.w. - dish (plate)	盘	pán
m.w. - grapes, bananas (bunch)	串	chuàn
m.w. - hat, cap	顶	dǐng
m.w. - newspaper, copy	份	fèn
m.w. - poem	首	shǒu
m.w. - rice, soup (bowl)	碗	wǎn
m.w. - room	间	jiān
m.w. - shoe, sock, animal	只	zhī
m.w. - shoes, socks (pair)	双	shuāng
m.w. - trousers, skirt	条	tiáo
magazine	杂志	zázhì
make	做	zuò

English	Simplified	Pinyin
man of one's father's age (*address*)	叔叔	shūshu
mandarin	橘子	júzi
map	地图	dìtú
market	市场	shìchǎng
match (*v.*)	配	pèi
may, can	可以	kěyǐ
meaning	意思	yìsi
meatballs (fried, or cooked with Chinese cabbage)	狮子头	shīzitóu
Melbourne	墨尔本	Mò'ěrběn
men's toilet	男厕	náncè
menu	菜单	càidān
midday, noon	中午	zhōngwǔ
middle school	中学	zhōngxué
midnight	半夜	bànyè
minute	分	fēn
Miss; young lady	小姐	xiǎojiě
Monday	星期一	xīngqīyī
monetary unit - cent	分	fēn
10 cents	角	jiǎo
10 cents [oral]	毛	máo
dollar	元 (圆)	yuán
dollar [oral]	块	kuài
money	钱	qián
M.S.G.	味精	wèijīng
month	月	yuè
more, a lot	多	duō
morning	上午	shàngwǔ
morning (early)	早上	zǎoshang
most	最	zuì
mother	母亲	mǔqin
mother's sister (in China)	姨	yí
(in Taiwan)	阿姨	āyí
movie	电影	diànyǐng
Mr.; husband	先生	xiānsheng
Mrs.; wife	太太	tàitai
multi-storey building	楼房	lóufáng

N

English	Simplified	Pinyin
nearly; fast; hurry	快	kuài
new	新	xīn
New York	纽约	Niǔyuē
newspaper	报纸	bàozhǐ
next month	下个月	xià gè yuè
next Sunday	下星期日	xià xīngqīrì
next week	下(个)星期	xià (gè) xīngqī

English	Simplified	Pinyin
next year	明年	míngnián
night, evening	晚上	wǎnshang
no problems	没问题	méi wèntí
not at all...	一点儿都不	yìdiǎnr dōu bù
not bad, pretty good [oral]	还不错	hái búcuò
not being courteous; not at all, you're welcome	不客气	bú kèqi
now, at present	现在	xiànzài
number	号码	hàomǎ
number; date	号	hào

O

English	Simplified	Pinyin
o'clock; dot	点	diǎn
often	常, 常常	cháng, chángchang
oh (surprise, understanding)	喔	ō
oh (realization)	哦	ò
oh no, how terrible [oral]	糟糕	zāogāo
old (nonliving things), worn	旧	jiù
Old Li	老李	Lǎo Lǐ
Old Wang	老王	Lǎo Wáng
on top of, above	上面	shàngmian
on, at, in	在	zài
one's heart's content	过瘾	guòyǐn
only	只有	zhǐyǒu
opposite (location)	对面	duìmian
or	还是	háishi
orange (colour)	橙色	chéngsè
order the food	点菜	diǎncài
outside	外面	wàimian

P

English	Simplified	Pinyin
pair [measure word]	双	shuāng
pick (someone) up	接	jiē
pineapple	菠萝, 凤梨	bōluó, fènglí
plain rice (in China)	米饭	mǐfàn
(in Taiwan)	白饭	báifàn
play chess	下棋	xiàqí
play; to dial	打	dǎ
play, to have fun	玩儿	wánr
please; invite	请	qǐng
plum; a surname	李	lǐ
poem	诗	shī
pretty	漂亮	piàoliang
primary school	小学	xiǎoxué
probably	大概	dàgài

English	Simplified	Pinyin
pull	拉	lā
purple	紫(色)	zǐ (sè)
push	推	tuī
put	放	fàng

Q

English	Simplified	Pinyin
queen	皇后	huánghòu

R

English	Simplified	Pinyin
rain (v.)	下雨	xiàyǔ
read	念	niàn
receive, reception	招待	zhāodài
red	红(色)	hóng(sè)
refrigerator	冰箱,	bīngxiāng,
	电冰箱	diànbīngxiāng
repair, fix	修理	xiūlǐ
restaurant	饭馆,	fànguǎn,
	餐馆,	cānguǎn,
	馆子	guǎnzi
return, come back	回来	huílai
rice (cooked)	饭	fàn
riddle	谜语	míyǔ
right (location)	右边	yòubian
right away	马上	mǎshàng
right, correct	对	duì

S

English	Simplified	Pinyin
same, together	同	tóng
San Francisco	旧金山	Jiùjīnshān
Saturday	星期六	xīngqīliù
say	说	shuō
school work, homework	功课	gōngkè
season	季, 季节	jì, jìjié
send	送	sòng
see, catch sight of	见	jiàn
seem, be like	好像	hǎoxiàng
self	自己	zìjǐ
sell	卖	mài
send to	送去	sòng qù
serve the rice	盛饭	chéngfàn
set, suit (m.w.)	套	tào
settle accounts	结帐	jiézhàng
shirt	衬衫	chènshān
shoes	鞋	xié
short (length)	短	duǎn
shorts	短裤	duǎnkù
should	该	gāi

English	Simplified	Pinyin
side	旁边	pángbian
sigh	唉	ài
simple meal [modest form]	便饭	biànfàn
sing	唱歌	chànggē
single-storey house	平房	píngfáng
sit	坐	zuò
sit anywhere	随便坐	suíbiàn zuò
skirt	裙子	qúnzi
sleep	睡, 睡觉	shuì, shuìjiào
slow	慢	màn
snow (v.)	下雪	xiàxuě
socks	袜子	wàzi
some other day	改天	gǎitiān
sometimes	有时,	yǒushí,
	有时候	yǒushíhou
soup	汤	tāng
sour	酸	suān
spare time	空	kòng
speak	说, 说话	shuō, shuōhuà
spring	春天	chūntiān
spring rolls	春卷	chūnjuǎn
steak	牛排	niúpái
still	还	hái
stop	停	tíng
strawberry	草莓	cǎoméi
street	街	jiē
study (n.)	书房	shūfáng
summer	夏天	xiàtiān
Sunday	星期日,	xīngqīrì,
	星期天	xīngqītiān
sunny day	晴天	qíngtiān
sweater	毛衣	máoyī
sweet	甜	tián
sweet and sour pork	古老肉,	gǔlǎoròu,
	咕噜肉	gūlūròu
swimming pool	游泳池	yóuyǒng chí
Sydney (used in China)	悉尼,	Xīní,
(used in Taiwan)	雪梨	Xuělí

T

English	Simplified	Pinyin
taichi	太极拳	tàijíquán
take to	带去	dài qù
talk; chat	谈	tán
teach (at school)	教书	jiāoshū
telephone	电话	diànhuà
telephone ringing sound	铃	líng

English	Simplified	Pinyin
television	电视	diànshì
television set	电视机	diànshìjī
temperature	气温	qìwēn
that's enough	好了好了	hǎo le hǎo le
then	那, 那么	nà, nàme
therefore	所以	suǒyǐ
thin, skinny	瘦	shòu
thought (mistakenly)	以为	yǐwéi
thunder shower	雷阵雨	léizhènyǔ
Thursday	星期四	xīngqīsì
tight-fitting (clothing); thin	瘦	shòu
time - concept	时间	shíjiān
time, moment	时候	shíhou
to, until	到	dào
today	今天	jīntiān
together	一起	yìqǐ
toilet	厕所	cèsuǒ
tomorrow	明天	míngtiān
too (exceedingly)	太	tài
torn, broken	破	pò
trousers, pants	裤子	kùzi
T-shirt	汗衫	hànshān
Tuesday	星期二	xīngqī'èr
twins	双胞胎	shuāngbāotāi

U

English	Simplified	Pinyin
under, below	下面	xiàmian
undershirt, T-shirt	汗衫	hànshān
university	大学	dàxué
urinate, urine	小便	xiǎobiàn
usually	平常	píngcháng

V

English	Simplified	Pinyin
vehicle, car	车	chē
very [oral]	挺	tǐng
video, video cassette	录像带	lùxiàngdài
visit	拜访	bàifǎng

W

English	Simplified	Pinyin
w.e. - obvious situation	嘛	ma
wait	等	děng
want; be going to	要	yào
warm	暖和	nuǎnhuo
washing machine	洗衣机	xǐyījī
watch (timepiece)	表	biǎo
water bed	水床	shuǐchuáng
wear (clothes, shoes etc.)	穿	chuān

English	Simplified	Pinyin
weather	天气	tiānqì
Wednesday	星期三	xīngqīsān
week	星期	xīngqī
weight - a unit = 0.5 kilograms	斤	jīn
welcome	欢迎	huānyíng
well-fitting (clothing)	合身	héshēn
Western-style attire, suit	西装	xīzhuāng
what happened, what's the matter	怎么回事	zěnme huí shì
what time	几点钟	jǐ diǎn zhōng
where	哪儿, 哪里	nǎr, nǎli
which one (person)	哪位	nǎ/něi wèi
which, what	哪	nǎ
white	白(色)	bái(sè)
White House	白宫	Báigōng
why	为什么	wèishénme
wife (used in Taiwan)	太太	tàitai
will; can, be ble to	会	huì
wind	风	fēng
windy	刮风	guāfēng
winter	冬天	dōngtiān
wish	祝	zhù
woman of one's mother's age (*address*)	阿姨	āyí
woman's dress (in China)	连衣裙	liányīqún
(in Taiwan)	洋装	yángzhuāng
women's toilet	女厕	nǚcè
word, character	字	zì
work, to work	工作	gōngzuò
worn	旧	jiù
write	写	xiě
write down	写下来	xiě xiàlai
wrong, incorrect	错	cuò

Y

English	Simplified	Pinyin
yellow	黄(色)	huáng(sè)
yesterday	昨天	zuótiān
you [polite form]	您	nín
yumcha	饮茶	yǐnchá

Z

English	Simplified	Pinyin
zero	零	líng

Answers to the riddles on page 40:

1. 天 2. 星 3. 早 4. 字

Appendix 3

LEARN TO WRITE
by lesson

Chinese		English
1 月	yuè	month; the moon
日	rì	day; the sun
号	hào	date; number
今	jīn	present (time)
明	míng	bright
昨	zuó	yesterday
天	tiān	day; sky
星	xīng	star
期	qī	a period of time
对	duì	right, correct
错	cuò	wrong, incorrect
可	kě	may, approve
以	yǐ	to use
行	xíng	all right; O.K.; to walk
生	shēng	to be born, to give birth to; pupil
2 在	zài	[in progress]; at, on, in
做	zuò	to do, to make
看	kàn	to read, to look at, to watch
书	shū	book
写	xiě	to write
字	zì	character, word
现	xiàn	now, present
点	diǎn	o'clock; dot
分	fēn	minute; cent
半	bàn	half
了	le	[grammatical word]
下	xià	latter part; under
午	wǔ	noon, midday
早	zǎo	early; morning
晚	wǎn	late; evening, night
3 哪	nǎ	where, which, what
儿	ér	[word ending]; son
前	qián	front, before
面	miàn	[word ending - location]; face

Chinese		English
后	hòu	behind, after
右	yòu	right (location)
边	biān	[word ending - location]; side
左	zuǒ	left (location)
里	lǐ	inside
外	wài	outside
回	huí	to return; [measure word]
来	lái	to come
怎	zěn	how
事	shì	business, matter
见	jiàn	to see
4 穿	chuān	to wear
衣	yī	clothes
服	fú	clothes
先	xiān	first
太	tài	too (exceedingly)
黑	hēi	black
白	bái	white
红	hóng	red
黄	huáng	yellow
蓝	lán	blue
绿	lǜ	green
色	sè	colour
件	jiàn	[measure word for clothes]
呢	ne	[question word]
找	zhǎo	to look for
5 多	duō	many, much, more
少	shǎo	few, little, less
钱	qián	money
买	mǎi	to buy
卖	mài	to sell
块	kuài	dollar
毛	máo	10-cent unit
到	dào	to arrive, to go to

Chinese		English
样	yàng	appearance
还	hái	also, still
要	yào	to want;
		to be going to
给	gěi	to give
谢	xiè	to thank
本	běn	[measure word for books, magazines etc.]
共	gòng	together

6

Chinese		English
空	kòng	free time
玩	wán	to play, to have fun
住	zhù	to live
电	diàn	electricity
话	huà	speech
请	qǐng	please; to invite
问	wèn	to ask
进	jìn	to enter
等	děng	to wait
出	chū	to go/come out
时	shí	time, hour
间	jiān	within (time/space); [measure word for room]
该	gāi	should
走	zǒu	to go, to leave, to walk
再	zài	again

7

Chinese		English
伟	wěi	great
兰	lán	orchid
起	qǐ	to rise
您	nín	[polite form] you
李	Lǐ; lǐ	a surname; plum
位	wèi	[measure word for person]
叔	shū	one's father's younger brother
候	hòu	time
游	yóu	to swim
泳	yǒng	swim
城	chéng	town
双	shuāng	pair

Chinese		English
功	gōng	skill, effort
夫	fū	man
鞋	xié	shoes

8

Chinese		English
因	yīn	cause, reason
为	wèi	for
所	suǒ	so; place
常	cháng	often, usually
馆	guǎn	shop, building
子	zi; zǐ	[suffix]; son, child
饮	yǐn	to drink
茶	chá	tea
都	dōu	all
平	píng	flat, even
客	kè	guest
气	qì	manner; air
米	mǐ	uncooked rice
炒	chǎo	to stir-fry
得	de	[degree, result of]

9

Chinese		English
雨	yǔ	rain
雪	xuě	snow
刮	guā	to blow (wind)
风	fēng	wind
热	rè	hot
冷	lěng	cold
凉	liáng	cool
春	chūn	spring
夏	xià	summer
秋	qiū	autumn, fall
冬	dōng	winter
北	běi	north
京	jīng	capital
暖	nuǎn	warm
阴	yīn	cloudy
晴	qíng	sunny
最	zuì	the most
高	gāo	high
低	dī	low
度	dù	degree